T0149405

How to Play Golf in a Single Plane

or, The Original Swing in Golf -
Learn it, Play it and Score with it!

BILLY J. GAINES SR.

Natural Golf Teacher of the Year "2001"
Natural Golf Certified Instructor "Jan 1998 –"Oct 2012"
World Golf Teachers Federation Top 60 Teachers "2006
USGTF Master Teaching Professional "1998"
The Heritage Registry of "WHO'S WHO" 2007-2008
Natural Golf's Platinum Teaching Award "2008"
Golf Right Golf Academy "2003"

authorHOUSE®

AuthorHouse™
1663 Liberty Drive
Bloomington, IN 47403
www.authorhouse.com
Phone: 1-800-839-8640

© 2014 Billy J. Gaines Sr.. All rights reserved.

No part of this book may be reproduced, stored in a retrieval system, or transmitted by any means without the written permission of the author.

Published by AuthorHouse 10/06/2014

ISBN: 978-1-4969-3770-4 (sc)
ISBN: 978-1-4969-3768-1 (hc)
ISBN: 978-1-4969-3769-8 (e)

Library of Congress Control Number: 2014915871

Any people depicted in stock imagery provided by Thinkstock are models, and such images are being used for illustrative purposes only.
Certain stock imagery © Thinkstock.

This book is printed on acid-free paper.

Because of the dynamic nature of the Internet, any web addresses or links contained in this book may have changed since publication and may no longer be valid. The views expressed in this work are solely those of the author and do not necessarily reflect the views of the publisher, and the publisher hereby disclaims any responsibility for them.

CONTENTS

DEDICATION

This book is dedicated to my beautiful bride of 49 years "Penny"; my one and only love! For all these years, she has stood by me with the greatest support anyone can ever ask for. She has always encouraged me in anything I have tried to do. If not for her and her encouragement, I know I would not be able to be who I am. She is the love of my life and she and my family are the only thing more important to me than my love of teaching golf.

I love you, Tweet.

The Original Swing in Golf - Learn it, Play it and Score with it!

Learn the original golf swing and how to use it efficiently.

Learn how to make the set up.

Learn how to make a repeatable swing - with power.

Learn how to take the golf swing from the driving range to the golf course.

Learn how you can have a more consistent ball flight with less body movements.

Learned golf from the driver through the putter and all the shots in between.

Learn how *not* to score big numbers.

Learn the fastest way to reduce you Handicap.

Learn how to play Golf and not have your back hurt!

Learn how to hit a straight ball flight.

All you have to do to learn all the above is, want to!

FOREWORD

The Beginning of Golf
Or
"How the Game of Golf got its start"

MR. PUNCH'S FANCY PORTRAITS.

RIGHT HON. ARTHUR GOLFOUR, M.P.
As Irish Secretary known to fame,
Golfour, links-eyed, pursues his favourite game.

While investigating the history of golf, various legends comes to light - no one knows for sure. The following is such a legend that when taken in full - sounds very plausible. I am not saying the following legend is actual fact but; then again, it may very well be, so as legend would have it;

In the early to mid-1400s a Scottish sailor was waiting for his buddies on the shoreline to disembark from their ship and join him to have some brews at the local pub. After waiting for a while he picked up a stick with a knot on the end of it and started swinging it like it was a big hammer and started hitting rocks into the water, "the first golf swing and the first golf club!"

Fascinated with the fact he could actually hit the rocks with this funny looking stick, he started to see how far he could hit them into the water, "the first golfer!"

When his buddies finally came ashore, he just tossed a stick into the bushes and frankly, forgot about it. As fate would have it, sometime later he was again alone in the same spot on the beach and waiting for his buddies.

Remembering what he had done before to pass the time, he looked for and found the same stick he had thrown into the bushes and started hitting rocks again, this time when his buddies approached, he just kept hitting the rocks into the water. At first his buddies, being the sea-faring type, started to ridicule him on the fact he was hitting rocks with a stick - but then, all of a sudden with their competitive spirit, one of his buddies found another funny looking stick and also started to hit rocks into the water. After a while, he tried to see if he could hit them further than his buddy," the first golf game!"

Soon, this phenomenon grew and grew until these sailors were making plans on getting to the shoreline just to hit rocks with the two sticks. Not wanting to share, while out to sea they started carving and shaping their own sticks into different shapes in order to be able to hit the rock farther. The first man-made golf clubs!

They also found that by hitting rocks or shells with their favorite stick that they had put so much work in, they would sometimes break them. This being so, they experimented trying to find just the right rock they could hit a long way and still not break their stick. Unfortunately, they could not find a rock that would not break their stick after being hit a few times. On their ship, they had the buckets of clay they used along with old sails or rope to fill cracks in the deck of the ship. Also knowing that sometimes the warships would use clay balls that was hardened for farter in their cannons, they decided to make small balls out of the clay and try them instead of rocks, "the first golf ball!"

They found that although the clay got hard, after a few hits by their custom made sticks they seemed to come apart. Next they looked around to see if they could find something that would keep the clay from falling apart when struck. They tried a lot of things but none of them did the job until one day one of them found on board some worn-out sails. They cut and wrapped it around the wet clay balls. They arranged the balls so they would harden in the sun.

Knowing the Scotts the way they are, along with them also being sailors, one of them came up with the idea of using their newfound game to see how many times it would take them to hit it to the pub. They started betting each other on who could get to the pub with the least amount of hits.

Because the first golfers had trouble remembering all their hits it took them to get to and especially from the pub back to the shore, they decided to separate this game into different challenges. To do this, they found sticks and stuck them in the ground. They would simply go from one post to the other until they reached the pub. This also gave them more chance to gamble and more drinks to win. This went along okay for a while, except they kelp losing sight of the stick they were playing to - especially after a visit to the pub. One of the guys said he could fix that problem and tied a piece of a worn-out sale to the top of each stick, "the first golf flag pole!

They experimented with how many post to put in the ground and eventually decided on seven. Seven seem like a very easy number to remember and besides the odd number broke all ties. All went well until the sea grass between the beach and the pub started growing, which made for another problem. How could they see their homemade ball and all the grass, especially around the pole? One ingenious sailor came up with a solution; he made arrangements to have a sheep farmer stakeout one of his sheep around every poll, "the first golf course!"

This newfound game did not go unnoticed by the ship's officers. First they tried to ignore it, then they tried to ban it because the use of the clay and the old sails which was felt they needed for ships store's, none of which succeeded until the captain got involved and assigned the midshipman to look into this new game and report back. As legend would have it, the midshipman got intrigued with the competition and reported back to the captain that he felt no harm was coming to the ship's crew as part of this new game. He said it looks to him as if the crew was establishing a new competitive nature along with learning how to count and be truthful and besides, the longer they played the game on shore, the less time they had to stay in the pub. The captain ordered the officers not to interfere. At this time, the game was known as a peasants game; not worthy of officers and gentlemen.

After listening to the crew talk about their newfound game, one of the officers asked if he could hit the ball with one of their sticks. Just as the crew, this officer got hooked on the game. Feeling it was beneath his dignity to make his own sticks and his own balls, he hired one of the crew to do it for him, "the first professional club maker!"

Before long, a lot of the officers aboard ship were having their individual clubs and balls made by their crew and like the crew, started playing and enjoying this newfound game. This was a big leap for the game of golf because the ship's officers introduced it to other ship's officers and it was finally integrated into the upper society and eventually spread throughout Scotland, Ireland and the United Kingdom. The game became so popular to the Aristocrats' that at one time the King of Scotland banned the game. He felt like his Knights were not paying enough attention to their Knightly skills and therefore weakened the defense of his kingdom.

From that point on, golf continued to grow, not only regionally and nationally, but worldwide. From its humble beginning on the Scottish seashore to being enjoyed by hundreds of millions of players in almost every country in the world. From almost every point on the globe, someone is hollering "fore"! It has truly become one of the best sports of all time. It is such an enthusiastic sport that every golfer becomes an instructor! What I mean by that statement is, say a person has only been playing golf for two months will try to teach somebody that's only been playing for one month. It seems to be such an emotional sport that people can't stop themselves from helping their fellow golfers even though most of the time it's not being asked for.

Now this just didn't happen overnight, it probably took many years to complete. Like I said, no one knows for sure, but it sounds good, "doesn't it"?

Golf has progressed through many stages in its evolution from a sailor picking up a stick hitting rocks on the seashore, to Scottish Knights, to the British nobles, on to the modern-day game available to all. Just as a game of golf went through many stages, so has the golf swing and the golf equipment. One of the major breakthroughs in the game of golf was when the golf club started being forged out of brass and copper. These clubs were used for years before steel was introduced into the game of golf, mainly used in the club head. The same can be said about the golf shaft and the grips. The grips went from bare wood to tar and leather, right to the modern-day grip we have today. They come in varying styles and texture, from a tapered to non-tapered, from soft to firm. Likewise, the shafts have also come a long way, from a wooden stick someone found lying on the ground, to specialize hickory, to steel and the modern-day shafts made of graphite.

Just as equipment and the game have come a long way, so has the golf swing. From a Scottish sailor picking up a stick off the ground and swinging it as if he would swing an axe or big heavy hammer, (using a single plane) to over the years trying to produce more club head speed by moving it out of the palms of the hands and into the fingers, creating the conventional swing. It is long been the consensus in the golfing world that the ball will go further using the conventional swing than using the single plane swing. To me that point is still up for debate but for arguments sake let's say it is so. As all good instructors will tell you the further the ball goes in the air the harder it is to control, this is also up for debate. To me control comes from the swing not the length of the ball flight. *"All that matters is the club face being square to the target line and moving down that target line with accelerating club head speed at moment of impact"*. A small sentence with a lot of meaning. As Mr. Norman has said many times the ball don't care who you are, how old you are, your gender are your race, it only cares about how the club head strikes it!!! That being so, doesn't it make sense to use the swing that will return that club head back to the ball as described above more consistently? And I contended is the new single plane swing and setup reinvented by Mr. Moe Norman!

BIOGRAPHY

"WHO AM I" and what makes me think I'm qualified to write this BOOK?

I was born in Mobile, Alabama in 1944. Throughout my life I have played many different sports and games—from hunting, fishing, football, and softball as a youth—to archery, chess, and bass fishing as an adult. When I was young in the Deep South, golf was a sport that only the well-to-do or privileged had a chance to enjoy. If I had told the people I was raised with that I would be a golf professional when I grew up, I may not have made it to adulthood! Boy, how things have changed!

I joined the Marine Corps when I was 17. The Corps instilled in me that I must always do the best job no matter what I do. This has guided me throughout my life, especially in the most challenging sport I have ever tried—golf.

I was introduced to golf by my father when I was 32 years old and played my second round when I was 36. Since golf is an individual sport and so challenging, I immediately got hooked. Because of my nature and training, I could not (as we say in the Marine Corps) "half-step." I bought a second-hand set of J.C. Penney "fiberglass" golf clubs, (which I didn't keep very long) and set out to learn how to play without any formal instruction. I have always been a pretty good athlete and a very good mimic. After watching pros like Tom Weiskopf and Jerry Pate swing the golf clubs I did my best to imitate them. After 10 years, I managed to get my handicap to a six.

By then, I had hit a plateau in my golf, so I finally sought a good pro and took a series of lessons. I only completed three of the five lessons, for the pro was only telling me what I already knew but did not have the confidence to perform. I feel sure that if I had taken the lessons before all the years of struggling I would have reached and passed this plateau years sooner. But just like everyone else, I didn't think at the time that I needed help, so I spent 10 years "beating myself in the head." Although I am the type of person who cannot accept mediocrity in my own performance, I do not judge anyone else, for they alone must judge themselves. All I can do is try to help my students become the best golfers they would like to be; it is their decision, I can only help.

I have been married 49 years to my beautiful bride Penny. We have raised four children and as of this date we have 13 grandchildren. I started teaching golf to my children as they were growing up. All four played golf on the high school team, and this is where I fell in love with golf instruction. At this time, I was a mechanic in a can plant in Jacksonville Florida. At age 51, the company that I worked for downsized and put me into retirement. By that time, I had managed to get my handicap down to a two. This was the year I won the club championship at Pineview Golf and Country Club in MacClenny Florida. At this point, I was wondering what to do with the rest of my life. It was my wife who suggested that I do what I love to do, and that is teach golf. So I got my certification as a Teaching Professional in the United States Golf Teachers Federation in February of 1997 teaching the conventional golf swing. I then, however, had to make a personal decision—which did I want to be more, a player or a teacher? I chose to become a teacher of golf and give up considering myself a player. This is not a decision I took lightly, but rather a realistic one. In my heart, I knew that I would never be good enough as a player to make a living. But I did consider myself good enough to teach and to help my students learn this great game. I must say that I have never regretted that decision; it was a turning point in my golfing career.

In January 1998, I received my certification as a Master Teaching professional in the USGTF again teaching the conventional golf swing. When I was going through the Masters Certification program, I was introduced to the single plane swing by Mr. Dale Hanson. He invited me to participate in a certification class for Natural Golf in February 1998 that Mr. Ken Ellsworth and he were conducting. At that time, Ken was the director of golf instruction for Natural Golf. I was so taken by the simplicity and the consistency of the Single Plane swing that I felt that I had to be a part of it. I went to Myrtle Beach, South Carolina to teach under Mr. Ellsworth. I helped Ken teach two one-day schools and was elevated to "Level 2" Natural Golf Certified Instructor in May of 1998. Since that date, I have had the privilege of teaching more than 5000 students in over 1200 Natural Golf schools.

I was fortunate enough to be chosen the inaugural Natural Golf Teacher of the year for 2001. I was also privileged to become a member of the Natural Golf Education Committee and the Natural Golf Advisory Board. In 2006, I was selected as one of the Top 60 Teachers by the World Golf Teachers Federation. The Federation has over 38,000 members in 36 Countries. In 2008 I was awarded Natural Golf's New Platinum Teaching Award. In 2004 I established Golf Right Golf Academy for my local students not affiliated with Natural Golf. Under the banner of golf right golf Academy I branched out to five different cities in Northeast Florida Southeast Georgia.

In closing this personal introduction, all I can say is that I hope that my students become as excited about learning as I do about teaching, for teaching is my passion.

The Golfer and the Teaching Pro.

As golfers, we go through several stages in our golfing life. First, we think, "That game can't be that hard," so we go to a driving range to hit some balls or play our first round of golf. By the time we find out that the game is "that hard," we've made at least one good swing or one good shot. We think, "If I can do it one time, why can't I do it all the time?" Golf is such an individual sport and the challenge are so great, also with the human competitive spirit being as it is, we get hooked!

So we get some clubs and set out to master the game. We think it can't take that long. Little do we know! In most cases, we seek help only after years of frustration. Only then have we admitted to ourselves that we don't have all the answers. By this time, we have developed bad habits that will take a lot of time and hard work to overcome. This is where the teaching professional comes in. The teaching professional is a person who has dedicated his or her life to teaching the game of golf, and who has only one thing in mind, that is to help students become the best golfers they can be. With the teaching professional's help, the golfer can work out those bad habits. With the right technique and the right frame of mind, they can develop a repeatable golf swing. The teaching professional (in most cases) has set aside his or her game just to concentrate on their student's game and gauges their success only by the success of their students' game, which leads us to the single plane swing. Mr. Norman has developed a swing that is so simple that it's a pleasure to play and teach. The trail hand palm grip and single plane swing is much easier to learn and teach than the conventional swing. Once you learn the skills you need, you will be well on your way to playing your best golf. The drills that we teach were designed to help you learn these skills. Do the drills as directed and you will see how easy the swing is to learn, <u>but you have to do the drills the right way!</u>

Golf is the only game where there's no one to help you when you get on the course. Once you address the ball, the swing and the game are all up to you. You get all the credit for the good shots, and all the blame for the bad ones. There isn't any better feeling than a good round of golf, or a worse feeling than a bad one. There may only be a five or six stroke difference between the two rounds, but what a difference in how they make you feel. With this in mind, doesn't it make more sense to learn the simplest and the most effective swing in golf, and that is as I believe is the single plane swing!

To whom it may concern!

This Book was written to give back some of the things I have learned about the Single Plane Swing and the Game of Golf over the last 34 years.

It is simply here to give you, the student, another way learn this great game of GOLF.

I wrote this book by myself. I am not an expert in the English language, just doing the best I can. If you are expecting to see a professionally writhen book, then you came to the wrong place, I can't afford to hire someone to do it and wouldn't even if I could. This is me, not some ones ideal of who and/or what I should be.

I am truly sorry if some of you can't get by my lack of education. I do not have a college degree, but I do know the game of golf and the swing. If you need a professor to teach you golf by using the right English composition then that's not me!

I am simply a Golf Professional that writes the way he talks and means what he says. If you can't get pass my bad spelling and lack of good grammar, then maybe you need to read someone else's book. But if on the other hand, you would like to have someone that only has you and your game at hart and will do anything he can to make you a "Better Golfer", then that's me and my book.

Like I've said many times, I don't matter, the course don't matter. The only thing that matters is "YOU" and your game!

If you will like to comment about this book or anything PLEASE visit my web site at www.billygainessr.com. I will be glad to hear from you.

Thank You,.............Bill

INTRODUCTION

The Original Swing

The Single Plane Swing

In this book I will be putting on paper what I have learned while teaching over 1200 golf schools and over 10,000 Students. I have found in most cases that the simpler you can explain to subject, the easier it is for the student to learn. Therefore in this book, I will explain what I think is the simplest swing in golf, the single plane swing made popular by Mr. Moe Norman and Natural Golf. Every golfer is unique and I have found that a teacher cannot communicate with every student the same way. A good instructor will have some 15 to 20 different ways to explain every position, technique or fundamental they are trying to teach. Therefore, it is important to discover the background and interest of every student that they are trying to instruct. In this book I do not have that luxury, so I will simply try to put on paper the best results of my teaching. As stated before, there are many different ways to explain every situation in golf. I am not trying to say this is the only way, it is simply the best way I know of to teach and help the reader understand this complex rotary motion known as, "the golf swing".

In this book you will notice there's only three chapters that strictly pertains to the single plane swing. The remaining of the book deals with every aspect of playing the game of golf. As stated before I am a golf instructor first with a preference to the single plane swing. It is worth noting at this time that I got my Master credentials as a conventional instructor teaching the conventional golf swing and later converted to a single plane golf instructor. All other aspects of the game of golf that I teach in this book other than the true single plane swing chapters can be adapted to and used with the conventional swing. I sincerely hope you enjoy this book and in some small way I hope I will be able to help a golfer somewhere, play their best game. With that in mind, I humbly give you this book.

You don't need to know how to play golf in order to learn a good setup! But you will need to learn a good set-up, "TO PLAY GOOD GOLF"!

This is so" IMPORTENT" that I will be repeating it all throughout this Book!!!

How the play the Game of Golf

Only after learning how to hit a golf ball will the emphasis turn to learning how to play the game of golf. Hitting a golf ball and playing golf are not the same thing. Of course, one must be able to hit a golf ball before they can play golf. Just as Mr. Norman said about the longest walk in golf – that is from the practice tee to the first tee –, most golfers can't take their swing with them to the golf course. At this time it may be a good time to go and read the chapter on "How to take your swing from the Driving Range to the Golf Course." The next step in your learning will be the second phase of that chapter, so take time to review it. Now let's get started.

It doesn't matter how you get the ball from one target to the next target. There have been golf champions of all levels with all kinds of swings. Some are high-ball hitters, some are low-ball hitters, and some hit their ball from left to right or right to left. There has also been some golfers that use the single plane swing. Some of them are powerful, long-ball players while others are short hitters. The golf course does not care about how; it only cares about how many strokes golfers take.

When learning to play the game of golf, your practice must be on the game of golf, not on your golf swing. To play the game of golf, your practice must be on the target. Whether you are making a 1 foot putt or hitting a 300 yd. drive, the target is the point you are trying the hit with that swing. Golf is a target game! Specifically, you are trying to hit a spot on the course within a reasonable range of error. Because of this, the game can be divided into a series of target skills. Become reasonably proficient at hitting the ball at these targets and you will score well and be able to play any course in the world.

Golf course designers lay out their courses with targets in mind. They think of the course in terms of target (landing areas) from the tee and approach shots (landing zones) into the greens. Some will have targets in high-risk/high reward areas while others will be in low risk/low reward areas. Sand traps, water, and other hazards on the golf course are to put some psychological pressure into your game. However, if you as a golfer are ready with a good swing and the skills to hit targets on the course, this psychological pressure will be minimized. Being proficient at target skills mean for the most part that you can hit targets that are away from the hazards, therefore reducing the trouble you can get into. Hitting targets away from trouble translates to lower scores.

Once the basic skills have been acquired, we can start using them to our advantage. We can now structure our game into manageable distances that we can apply. Golf courses worldwide are all about direction and distance, within a certain degree of error. All we have to do basically is hit our target, and then we can logically and rationally play any course anywhere. To play good golf one must have the ability to hit the target, and hitting the target means hitting the ball the right distance and in the right direction.

Another point is that somewhere in the neighborhood of 50 to 60 percent of your scoring is in the short game on and around the greens. To focus on the distant target skills is to focus on the power game and so you should, but the money is in the short game. Just think, a 1 in. putt costs the same as a 300 yd. drive…. "One Stroke." So why not get proficient at all the skill levels, the power game and the short game? It takes less strain and less athletic ability to hit short shots to their targets, but this is of the part of the game that can quickly improve your scoring! I understand that there are physical limitations to the power game. Not everyone will be able to hit the 300 yd. drive, but I cannot accept any excuse why anyone cannot be proficient in the short game. It all comes down to this: to have a proficient short game, one must have the right techniques, tweak them to fit their own physical attributes, (if any) and have the willpower to practice them correctly.

Like I've said many times, practice with a purpose, practice with a goal, but most of all practice only one thing at a time!

Chapter 1

THE MENTAL GAME - GETTING PREPARED

Tension

When it comes to biomechanics, (the golf swing) tension is a killer—especially in the game of golf. It's almost impossible to make a good golf swing with tense or flexed muscles. Tension in the body was learned—you were not born tense; it took you years to learn. But just as you learned to be tense, you can learn to relax!

We need to first acknowledge that you probably didn't get tense during the swing, but rather during the setup, where most golfers have difficulty relaxing. This is good news, because it's easier to learn to relax during the setup than during the swing. In most cases, tension in the setup starts with the grip, and carries over into the swing. (You may need to review the section on grip pressure.) That being so, here is a mental exercise or drill that can be done very easily and will teach you how to relax.

Three times a day, put yourself into a relaxed state, anywhere you like, as long as you're not operating equipment or putting you or someone else in danger. Next, close your eyes and totally relax. While in this relaxed state, imagine yourself swinging a golf club five times. Only five times, for if you go past the five you will tend to start building tension. That's the opposite of what we're trying to achieve. Aim to do this three times a day for about three weeks; by that time you should notice that you are starting to relax during your setup, and that your swing will start to be more consistent and, most importantly, smooth.

Focus - Concentration

Being able to focus or concentrate is one of the most important aspects of the game of golf. But what is focus? It is merely the state of mind in which you blank out all that does not pertain to the task you are trying to accomplish, whether it be your job, driving a car, a sports endeavor—anything.

Unfortunately, most golfers do not have this ability, or cannot focus or concentrate long enough to last through the setup and the swing. Some think it is not necessary; other just don't know how. It makes no difference which it is—not having it will simply keep you from playing your best game. Obviously, the top players in the world have learned how to achieve that state of mind. You can too. Here's a way to teach yourself to focus by doing a mind drill.

Start with the relaxation drill. Three times a day put yourself into a relaxed state, anywhere you like as long as you're not operating equipment or putting you or someone else in danger.

Find a spot or some small object that is stationary, fix your eyes on that object, and concentrate on it for just five seconds. Create a state of mind where nothing around you matters except that small object. Do this often enough so that it becomes easy to achieve and maintain that relaxed, focused state. It usually takes on average about two weeks to maintain a relaxed focus for that first five seconds. Then increase to 10, 15, 20 and 25 seconds, each time moving to the longer period only when you can easily maintain focus for the current period.

25 seconds may not sound like much, but the average setup and address in golf only takes about 20 seconds for most people after they have learned the setup and pre-shot routine. The best golfers in the world can focus for up to one minute, which seems an eternity to most of us. If the top golfers seem to be out of touch with anything that's happening around them during their setup and swing, it's because they are! Some ask how the professional golfers can concentrate on their game for up to five hours at a time. The answer—they don't; they concentrate on their setup and swing one minute at a time.

NOTE: All throughout this book I will be referring to the <u>Six Timing Positions of the single plane Golf Swing</u>. This info is in chapter 4, section B. You may need to look at it from time to time.

Focus on execution, not results

One of the biggest flaws a golfer can make is to focus on results instead of concentrating on execution. If a golfer focuses on results and not on execution the results may or may not be accomplished. This is like what has been said as, putting the horse behind the cart. Until the golfer has practiced enough to make execution automatic, the focus should always come after execution. When this happens, the results the golfer is looking for will become more frequent.

To play the Game of Golf

To play the Game of Golf all one must know is, how to move a ball from one place to the other using the least amount of strokes.

This can be accomplished by knowing how to move the golf club from the pre-impact to the full extension as seen below! All the time making sure the club face remains square to the swing plane and using the maximum club head speed the golfer can control. This is all that matters! If this is simple for you, do not read any further, go out and play this Great Game and LOVE IT. If not, please move through this book slowly making sure you understand what you have read before going to the next. The worst thing I think one can do when trying to learn anything is, getting too anxious to know and moving too fast, ***"Slow down Please"***.

You cannot manipulate the golf swing

Since we were born we have tried to manipulate everything that we do, now you must realized you cannot manipulate the golf swing, you have to just let it happen. To get a proper golf swing you must think of two words. 1st word is "D R I L L", 2nd word is "S W I N G". They are not spelled the same, they are not pronounced the same and they don't have the same meaning. The DRILLS are not the SWING but only a small part of it, No one has ever learned the DRILLS by making a SWING but you can only learn the SWING by doing the DRILLS. To learn the SWING you must practice each drill *slowly*, until it becomes second nature then go to the next drill. This is the time to think about it; to make the SWING you must not think of the DRILLS, only the swing. If the swing is not there then go back to the DRILLS. To play the game of golf you cannot think about the golf swing, you must think "TARGET". If you have practiced the drills enough the right way you will have the confidence that the golf swing will be there so that you can focus on the TARGET.

Learn the DRILLS *slowly* to get to the SWING.

Practice the SWING to get the ball to the TARGET.

Think TARGET to play GOLF!

Drills or Swing

First, let's explore some things one must know before trying to learn a golf swing - little things that if known will make your learning easier and faster. As stated before there are two words to remember; these words are "D R I L L S" and "S W I N G". Do not confuse these two words. You have to do the drills very slowly in the conscious mind to build the memory in your subconscious mind. By performing drills accurately in your conscious mind, you can transfer the learning to the subconscious mind. In other words, do the drills slowly so that you can make the swing fast.

The mind can and will play tricks on you if you don't pay attention. It will give you what you ask for; you have to be able to ask for the right things. What feels good to you may not be the correct things to achieve the moves we are working on. More than likely, if you are trying to change and the change feels well to you, it's usually wrong.

I keep hearing some instructors and players use the term "muscle memory". There is actually no such thing as muscle memory. The only memory you have is found between your ears. The learning process in the brain is very unique. The way the brain learns biomechanics is through the conscious mind, "slowly". The conscious mind will only analyze data in one-second increments, while the subconscious part of the brain can operate in increments of milliseconds.

Let us use this example to explain I'm trying to say. Think about how long it would take you to get on a bicycle and ride away if before you did it you had to think of everything you needed to do to ride that bicycle-every movement, every balance, and every leverage point. You would have to think about everything your body was doing: where your hands and feet and arms were; where and how to move them; how to adjust the bike and stay in balance; then where and how to put your feet on the pedals and how to grab the handlebars. Along with hundreds of other things to think about before you actually did them. All this just to be able to ride that bike.

I don't know about you, but it would probably take me over an hour, and then I'd still probably fall.

Let's take this bicycle analogy even further. How did you learn to ride a bicycle? Once you learned to get on a bicycle, someone had to hold you on the bicycle until you learned how to balance yourself. When you learned how to balance yourself, whoever was holding you would give you a slight shove and you were on your way. The next thing they would explain is how to guide or steer the bicycle using the handlebars. Once you got good at that, they would introduce the pedals. They would show you how to move your feet and make the bike go forward. Then they would show you how to move the pedals backward to slow or stop the bike (we're talking about the old-style bike now, the one with coaster brakes). After you learned how to pedal, make the bike go forward, and how to apply the brakes, you must have been thinking, "Boy I'm getting good." And you did well until you got to the end of the street and realized you did not know how to turn around. "Back to the drawing board" now someone has to teach you how to lean into the turn while moving the handlebars. Now you are well on your way. In just a little while after learning how to ride the bike, you were running through mud puddles, jumping ramps, and having a good time.

Just like the bicycle, you have to learn the golf swing one step at a time. You do this through DRILLS. You must learn the drills one by one and completely before moving to the next. The trick is knowing which drill to learn first and in what order to do the rest. In golf, you should learn a good sound setup, and only then learn to swing. After you have learned the swing, then and only then should you learn how to play golf.

To get a proper golf swing you have to practice drills <u>slowly</u>, and think about what you're doing until it becomes second nature. To play the game, you cannot think about the golf swing, you must have practiced the drills enough (and have the confidence) that the golf swing will be there.

As I said before, most people want to play golf before they learn how to swing. They want to learn how to swing before they learn a good setup. This is absolutely the opposite way of learning golf. Playing golf is different than learning how to make a golf swing. And making a golf swing is different than learning a good setup. Do the steps in reverse and your evolution in golf will be much faster and more enjoyable. Everyone would like to hit the ball consistently, but unfortunately only a few will take the time to learn the setup and swing correctly and wonder why they cannot. Please don't let that be you!

Fastest way to reduce your handicap

The fastest way to reduce your handicap is simply played to your handicap. Let me explain, this example is going to be based on a golfer with a 12 handicap. How do you get an official USGA handicap card? The USGA, the official ruling body of golf in the United States issues the golfer their handicap based on how they score on their last 20 rounds of play. For this example the golfer has a USGA handicap of 12. In stroke play is their actual score -12. This gives the golfer their net score. In match play on the 12 lowest handicap holes on a golf course, the golfer gets one stroke. The fastest way to reduce your handicap? Once again, you are playing a mental game with yourself so always play match play in your head. If the number one handicap hole is a par five, then for you with a stroke it is your par six, play to it. If you get a six on that hole with your handicap you have a par. On the other hand, if you get a five on that hole do you have a par? "No you have a birdie"! Ask yourself, "What happens when I shoot birdies?" Your handicap goes down as long as the remaining holes are played to your par. What happens if I shoot a six? Nothing; that is your par. What happens if I shoot a seven? You have a bogey, not a double bogey. So as you can see, if you play to your handicap you can reduce it very rapidly. It's all in your mind, use it!

Chapter

2

BALL FLIGHT LAWS

To understand ball flight laws, we must first be thinking about the same things. Let me take the time to explain what we will be talking about. I know most golfers already know about these - but some may not – so with that in mind, lets get started. The first thing we need to do is look at the 9 flight paths in the picture below. To fully understand the ball fight laws you must know what the flights are called and then what makes the ball get there.

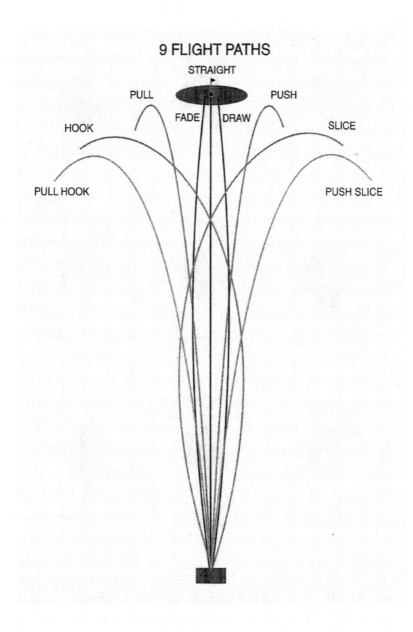

Study the picture above and it will make it simple to understand the name of each flight path and where it goes. This example is for a right-handed golfer lefties must reverse.

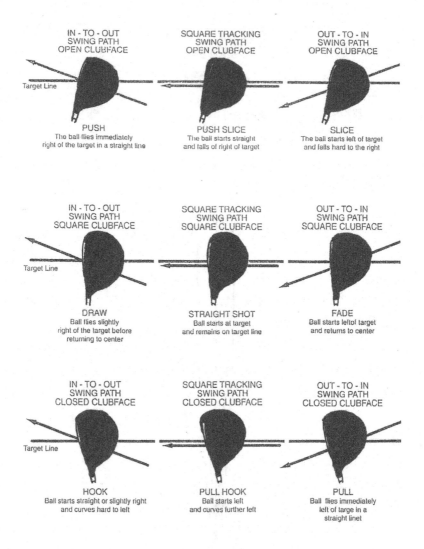

In the picture above, you can see that the target line is the direction where you want the ball to go and the arrow is the direction you are swinging the club (the path). The clubface is the angle the club is at when it impacts the ball. You can see that only one of these positions are correct and only it can produce a straight ball flight. If you will match the clubface above to the ball flight in the picture before, you can see what the clubface and the swing path looks like to produce that ball flight. Now that we know what we are trying to learn, let me go into greater detail.

Face

To hit a ball straight, at impact - the sole or bottom of the club must be flat to the ground (that is, touching the ground from heel to toe and from front to rear), and the face must be square to the target line with the club head moving down that target line and with the right amount of club head speed to send the ball, with backwards spin, to the target. This is very important, because if any one of these angles or positions of the clubface are out of alignment "at moment of impact," the ball will simply go off-line or out of trajectory. Let's diagnose these statements and see just what we're talking about.

Before you panic - let me tell you that the single plane swing and set-up makes these angles and positions for you if you have your clubs fitted to you and your swing is correct.

By placing a pointer or a square on the face of the club, you can see what direction and trajectory the ball will take off the face of the club.

Let's examine 'flat to the ground' more thoroughly.

Flat to the ground

Front to Rear   Heel to Toe

Heel to Toe

If you elevate the toe of the club off the surface, the direction of ball flight indicated by the square or pointer is to the left (a pull shot to the left or draw for a right-handed golfer).

By taking the heel off the ground instead, leaving the toe on the ground, the direction of ball flight indicated by the square or pointer is to the right (a push shot to the right or fade for a right-handed golfer).

Front to Rear

If the shaft of the club is behind the club head (see the left picture), you will notice that the pointer or square will produce a higher ball trajectory, because you have increased the loft. For example, an 8-iron held in this position may produce the same loft as a 9-iron.

In the middle picture, you will notice that the shaft of the club is pointed very slightly forward (toward the target), not straight up. In this position, the hands should be ahead of (or leading) the club head through impact. If you do this, you will ensure the right trajectory and, most importantly, acceleration of the club head through impact. An 8-iron will then produce a proper 8-iron loft.

If you take the shaft of the club and move it more forward of the club head (as in the right picture), you will notice that the pointer or square indicates a lower loft or trajectory. An 8-iron may then produce the loft of a 7-iron.

Now I hope it is clear why it's important to keep the sole flat on the ground (or surface) from heel to toe and front to rear at the moment of impact.

Square to the Line

A club head is square to the line when its face is 90 degrees from the intended line of flight (or what is known as the target line) and the sole of the club is flat to the ground at the moment of impact.

Billy J. Gaines Sr.

The Straight Ball Flight

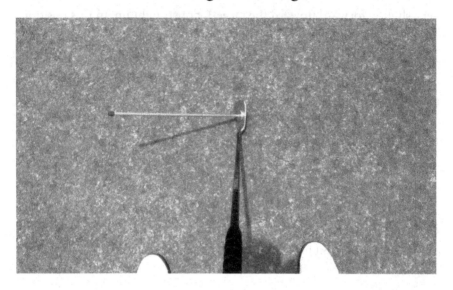

If (a) the sole of the club is flat on the ground (or surface) from heel to toe and front to rear, (b) the path of the swing marries the target line at the moment of impact, and (c) the face of the club is square to the target line, the ball will fly straight and true to its target. As stated before, if any of these angles or positions of the clubface are out of alignment "at moment of impact," the ball will simply go off-line or out of trajectory.

NOTE: In the following pictures, the black line is the target line and the red line is the swing path.

Square Face – Straight Path

"This is the only face and path that will give you a straight ball flight."

As mentioned earlier, the first curve of a well-struck ball is the continuation of its initial trajectory (up). The next two possible curves are either left or right. When a golf ball is on the ground and the bottom of the club is in line with the bottom of the ball, the power point on the face of the club will be below the balls equator. If the club head strikes the ball on a descending path before the club head contacts the ground, that swing will create the desired backwards spin. (Spin will be explained fully in chapter 4.)

If the toe of the club is in front of the heel of the club at impact of the ball, the clubface will be in - what is called - a closed position, impacting a sideways spin to the ball. This will make it curve to the left (for a right-handed golfer), which is called a "draw". On the other hand, if the heel of the club is in front of the toe, the clubface will be in an open position, impacting a sideways spin to the ball and make it curve to the right (for a right-handed golfer), called a "fade".

NOTE: The only difference between a draw and a hook, and between a fade and a slice, is how far the clubface is closed or open at impact. The more the clubface is off square, the more the ball will curve.

Closed Face – Toe in front of the heel

As stated before - if the heel the club is behind the toe at moment of impact, the spin of the ball will be tilted on an axis to the left side, for right-handed golfers, reflecting the face of the club. Therefore, the ball will curve in flight and make the ball draw or hook depending on how far the face is in the closed position. In this position, the ball flight will have a lower trajectory because the club will be de-lofted. In other words, the more the club is closed, the less loft there is on the clubface making for a lower ball flight. If this happens, then it matters not what number club you are using, it will be de-lofted making it go longer. To put it another way – a 7-iron may become a 6-iron flight path.

Open Face – Toe behind the heel

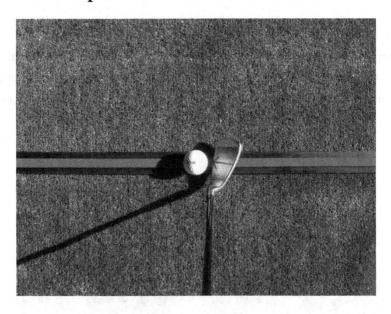

If the toe of the club is behind the heel of the club at moment of impact, the spin of the ball will be tilted on an axis to the right side, for right-handed golfers, reflecting the face of the club. Therefore, the ball will curve in flight and make the ball fade or slice depending on how far the face is open. In this position, the ball flight will have a higher trajectory because the club will have more loft. The more the clubface is open, the more loft there is on the clubface and the higher the ball flight. If this happens, then it matters not what number club you are using because it will be putting loft on the club making it go higher and shorter. To put it another way – a 7-iron may become an 8-iron flight path.

As stated, spin is what makes the ball go straight or curve to the right or left. When the clubface is out of alignment at moment of impact, it creates not a backward spin, but a sidespin on an angle relative to the face of that club, either the right or left. How far? That depends on how far the face of the club is out of alignment at impact.

PATH

Now let me explain about path! Path is the direction you swing the golf club though the impact zone. In the pictures below, remember that the black line is the target line and the red line is the swing path. As we go further in this book, I will cover the reason why the path is where it is but for now let us concentrate only on its direction.

Slice

Above in this pictures you can see that the swing path is - what is called – from outside to inside swing path. This is normally made by an over the top swing – which is explained in chapter 6 of this book. If you look at the pictures on the nine flight paths, you will see that only the path has changed and that alone will make the ball flight change.

Above in this picture you can see that the swing path is - what is called – from inside to outside swing path. This is normally made by a shoulder alignment or a weight transfer problem – which again is explained in chapter 6 of this book. Again, only the path has changed and that alone will make the ball flight change.

To recap, all of these examples are for the right-handed golfers; lefties must reverse the directions.

If both the face and path is correct but you elevate the toe or heel off the surface at impact, the direction of ball flight will be out of alignment to the target line.

If the shaft of the club is out of alignment, (front to rear) at impact it will cause the ball to be out of trajectory.

If the clubface is out of alignment at impact, the ball will spin on an axis to reflect the face of the club.

Chapter 3

THE "IMPACT ZONE"

To play the game of golf, all one must know is how to move a ball from one place to the other using the least amount of strokes.

To best understand the impact zone we need to know what we are trying to accomplish in that zone. To make a ball fly straight along the target line, when the club gets to the impact position the swing path and the target line must marry. The single plane setup and swing will allow that to happen more consistently. At the same time, the club head must be square to the target line. The single plane grip will allow this to happen more consistently.

This can be accomplished by knowing how to move the golf club from the pre-impact to the full extension as seen below! All the time making sure the club face remains square to the swing plane and using the maximum club head speed the golfer can control. This is all that matters! If this is simple for you, do not read any further, go out and play this great game and LOVE IT. If not, please move through this book slowly making sure you understand what you have read before going to the next. The worst thing I think one can do when trying to learn anything is, getting too anxious to know and moving too fast, "Slow down please".

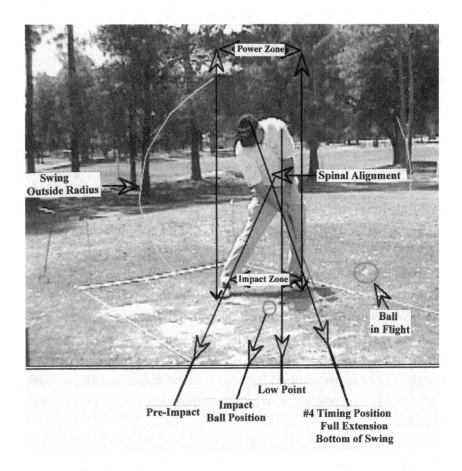

The Nomenclature of the Impact & Power Zone

In this chapter we will only be explaining the parts of the impact and power zones, not their functions. How to achieve the motions will be explained in later chapters.

What we are trying achieve when it comes to hitting a golf ball is to make sure the face of the club does certain things through the impact zone. It is important to remember that everything we do in the setup and swing has one purpose - to achieve the correct clubface alignment moving through the impact zone. To better understand this zone, let's divide it into three different areas. The first area is from the trail foot to the ball position. This area is known as <u>pre-impact</u>. Ball position (where the ball is on the ground and the club impacts the ball) is also known as the <u>impact position</u>. Where the club head meets a point in line with the lead foot is known as the <u>#4 timing position.</u>

The main objective of any golf swing is to get the impact zone and the power zone to become one! The perfect position of both the impact zone and the power zone is from in front of the big toe of the trail foot to in front of the big toe of the lead foot. Not all golfers will be able to achieve these positions, but they should try to get as close to them as they can.

I will explain the impact zone in this chapter, and then explain the power zone in a later chapter. At that time, we will put them together so that you can become a golfer who swings with power and distance.

The impact zone is the area between the feet that consists of three positions, which are: pre-impact, impact (or what is better known as ball position), and the #4 timing position, also known as the bottom of the swing or full extension.

The low point of the swing is not a timing position. Instead, it is just a position where the golf club gets to the lowest point in the swing relative to the ground (see later description of this low point). As long as the ball is being hit off the ground, that low point will always be about two inches **forward** of the ball position. See ball position in the diagram.

This is not meant to make things confusing, but to try to help golfers understand why these positions are where they are, and why they are named the way they are.

The power zone is where the arms extend and the wrists release (uncocking), letting the head of the golf club accelerate to its fullest velocity. The arms get to their fullest extension upon reaching the #4 timing position.

Pre-impact

This first area is known as pre-impact. Pre-impact is an area from the trail foot to ball position. In this pre-impact area, we need to have the club head in the proper position so that it can do what we need it to do at impact.

Impact

Next is the only position that really matters, IMPACT!!! The impact position (or what is better known as ball position) is where the club and the ball come together to produce ball flight. It is important at this position that the club head be flat to the ground and square the target line, as stated before this is the only position that really matters. Everything we do in the complete setup and throughout the swing is designed to make sure that the club head is correctly placed at the impact position.

Low Point

It is important to repeat that the low point of the swing is not a timing position, but instead a reference point on the ground to establish the correct ball position. In moving around the body, the club head traces the shape (or path) of a circle. The low point of that circle is directly under its center (or pivot). In the single plane swing, that pivot point is the lead shoulder. The low point will therefore be directly under the lead shoulder. With this being so, ball position will only change in relationship to the low point when hit off a tee with a driver.

Bottom of the Swing

The next position, which is located just in front of the lead leg, will be known as the #4 timing position (also known as full extension, or the bottom of the swing).This is also the only position in the swing where the full extension of the arms and club should line up with the spine angle.(See the chapter on set-up)

Note: A golfer should always try to fully extend the arms and club at the #4 timing position, never at impact (see above picture). If the golfer 'swings to Impact,' the club head will reach its full acceleration <u>before</u> it gets to the ball. This is known as "swinging at the ball." If, however, the golfer swings to the bottom of the swing, the club head will accelerate <u>through</u> the ball. That's what gives your swing power and distance. Put the emphasis on the swing not the hit!

Power Zone

The power zone is the area in the golf swing where the club head accelerates to its maximum speed. How to produce power will be covered fully in chapter 5 of this book - for now all we are explaining is the power zone. In the single plane swing, force is also applied. The biggest changes I can see in the professional golf swing in the last 50 years is the way the pros have learned to apply force through their power zone. This is what Mr. Norman learned when he reinvented the single plane swing. It is said that with the traditional swing you need to try to keep the trail hand and arm out of the swing because can make you come over the top and slice the ball. In the single plane swing, the trail hand and arm are one of the main fundamentals that make the swing much simpler to learn and control.

The biggest mistake I see in all golfers – traditional and single plane swings - is that they try to hit the ball with as much power they can muster. This will never give the golfer the consistency they need to become a good golfer. What is needed to have the consistency and power is learn to make the swing and have the swing generate the power and have it accelerate through the ball. Sounds simple – well it can be if you approach it the right way. One must learn that <u>power</u> is not just muscle – but the mass and acceleration of the club head plus force. As stated before in this book you cannot keep muscle out of the golf swing, but you can easily put too much into it!

Generating maximum power <u>when impacting the ball</u> will give you the most energy transfer but the least amount of consistency. Take for instance the long ball driving professionals. They need to have their most power at impact so they try to have their maximum mass and acceleration of the club head plus force at moment of impact. But remember, <u>they have 5 shots</u> to get one in the landing area – <u>you as a golfer only have one</u>.

What is needed to have consistency is - to have the club head accelerating through impact - not to impact! The long drive pros have a power point they are trying to achieve. As a golfer - we must try to achieve a power zone not a power point. This is where learning about the power zone comes in.

I like to describe the swing into the power zone in the same terms as a jet fighter hitting its after-burner. The power zone is where the golf swing hits its after-burner and here is how it's done. The forward swing starts from the top of the back swing and continues to the finish. It gains in speed until the arms are fully extended at the #4 timing position. When the swing gets to the pre-impact position, the wrist are still in a cocked position - at which time they release and accelerates the club to it maximum power at the #4 timing position. The wrist release is the after-burner of the golf swing. What makes the release more powerful in the single plane swing versus the traditional swing, is that the <u>trail arm is extending through impact</u>. In the single plane swing, one of things that is taught is the trail arm must extend through impact – like what you would do when nailing a nail into a board with a hammer.

One of the questions I ask my students most about power is: If you were trying to drive a nail into a board what are you trying to hit with the hammer??? Most tell me it is the nail! I tell them if that were so you would never drive the nail into the board only bend it. To drive the nail into a board one must try to hit the board with the hammer and put the nail into its path. This is the same as either extension to or through the golf ball. Never try to hit a golf ball for power – drive the club though it to the target that will get you the power. Think of is way - the hammer is the golf club, the nail is the ball and the board is the #4 timing position, the target is where you want the ball to go. Now all you have to do to get your power is to marry your power zone to the impact zone, (make them the same) as in the picture – "Nomenclature of the Impact and Power Zone".

WHAT IS SPIN?

Spin is the rotation of the ball while in flight. When the clubface contacts the ball cleanly below its equator on a descending path, backwards spin will be applied to the ball. (Descending path can also be described as angle of approach).

It has been said that if you can control the spin of the ball, you can control its flight. This is so—let's explore why. Two things must be considered when talking about ball flight. The first is velocity and the second is spin. Velocity is the speed of the ball through the air (forward momentum). The second is the spin (rotation) of the ball.

Three things will happen to the ball when it is struck by a golf club: (1) the ball will start on a trajectory produced by the loft of the club, (2) the mass of the club and the speed of the club head will create velocity, and (3) the descending path of the club cleanly striking the ball below its equator will produce a backwards spin.

What does spin do to the ball in its flight and why?

When a golf ball has a backwards spin, it will produce lift. "NOTE" A golf ball struck clean and properly below its equator will start in its flight with the correct trajectory and with the maximum velocity and spin that the club head speed can produce. Backspin is when the ball is the rotating to the rear over the top. This backwards spin causes the bottom of the ball to move through the air faster than the top of the ball.

Think of it this way—the bottom of the ball is rotating into the direction of the ball flight and the top of the ball is rotating away from the ball flight direction. The velocity and spin builds more pressure at the bottom than at the top, causing the ball to move away from that pressure, thus creating lift and a rising trajectory. A golf ball will always move to the top of its spin.

Unlike what some may think, a golf ball can actually curve in four different directions: up, down, left or right (see ball flight laws chapter 2). Here is where spin comes into play. Only after the forward momentum slows does the spin of the ball have an effect on its flight. If the spin on the ball is a backwards rotation, the ball will curve straight up created by its lift which will give the illusion of a straight path. When the ball is contacted at its equator or above the ball, it will have an over the top spin which will drive the ball to the ground or in a low trajectory. This is known in the golfer's world as top spin.

For a golf ball to turn in its flight, some kind of side spin must have been applied. When a ball has a left or right side spin, it will curve in that direction. How that sideways spin is applied to the ball will was explained earlier in this book. This is why the modern day driver ball flight requires less spin.

NOTE: Without spin, the ball will only react to the direction of the club face at impact; but with spin the ball will react first to the swing path and then to the position of the club face relative to the ball (open or closed). So, the position of the clubface and the path of the club head is moving at impact is what makes the ball go in its direction!

SINGLE PLANE

The single plane swing was made popular by Mr. Moe Norman. Mr. Norman did not invent the single plane swing, but simply perfected it. In this book am not trying to get into Mr. Norman's head just explaining the motion and set-up he perfected.

I will repeat myself in various subjects because they are that important. This is one such subject!

There are four basic fundamentals in the single plane swing set up which are: single plane, stable stance, face the ball of impact and the trail hand palm grip. If I had to rate the single plane four fundamentals in order of importance I believe they are:

#1 the single plane, created by the set up and maintained throughout the swing.

#2 a stable stance, because it will help the golfer maintain good balance and posture in order to stay in the single plane.

#3 facing the ball at impact, because it will allow the golfer to swing down the target line more consistently and create more of the Square Tracking motion we are seeking in the impact zone.

#4 is the trail hand palm grip.

For a complete explanation of these four fundamentals see chapters on setup and/or drills.

What is the Single Plane?

The best definition of a single plane movement is a circular motion always in line with itself. In other words, the single plane is best compared to the pendulum motion. The shaft of a pendulum will move in a straight line back and forth while the weight on the end of that shaft will move in a circular motion. In the single plane golf swing, the golf club likewise will move in the same straight line as the pendulum while the head of the club will move in a circular motion as the weight of the pendulum. The picture below shows the single plane set-up with a driver and a 7-iron.

| Driver | 7 Iron |

As you can see, the axis of the plane has changed, but both setups are still in a single plane. Why does the plane change with different clubs? It doesn't! The single plane does not change only the axis it's on changes because the length of the shaft. NOTE: the longer the shaft, the more axis that is needed to maintain the single plane. So remember, just because the plane is tilted on a different axis does not mean it's not on a single plane. All this means is, when you are in these setups you will still be swinging on a single plane, just on different axes.

During the single plane swing, the golf club will move on the back swing in one axis and return on the forward swing on a different axis, but in the same single plane.

"Ah ha" you say! Now he's making the swing complicated, but that's not so. The single plane setup makes the alignment of the shoulders to be in a slightly closed position at address; this sets up the axis of the backswing. The backswing and forward swing are initiated by the shoulder movement. In other words, the single plane is controlled by the movements of the shoulders. Since the shoulders will moves first in the forward swing, they will automatically move from closed position to a squared position to the target line. So just remember that the shoulders at address and the shoulders at impact are not the same.

Note: the shoulder alignment will dictate the axis on which the arms move in that single plane. Although the axis will change during the swing because of the different shoulder alignment at setup and at impact, the single plane on which you swing will not!

A lot of golfers wonder why they pull or push the ball when using the single plane swing. Most of the off line hits can be traced to the shoulder alignment at impact. If the shoulders are square at address and make the proper swing with the shoulders rotating more than the hips, they will be in an open position at impact. Ask yourself, what makes the ball go in any direction? The ball will go in the direction that the club face is moving, the club face will move in the direction the shaft is moving, the shaft will move in the direction the hands are moving, the hands will move in the direction the arms are moving and the arms will move in the direction the shoulders are moving; it is a chain. As you can see, the shoulders are the main reason the ball goes off line. Not the only reason, but the major reason. As I have stated before, it's not where your shoulders are aligned at address that matters, only where your shoulders are aligned at impact.

Next, we move to the arms. The arms serve many functions in the single plane swing and setup such as angles, leverage and timing. None more important that achieving the correct angles in the setup for a single plane swing. We will only be talking about the setup position of the arms in this chapter.

Although some think both arms together form a single plane, this is not accurate. To start with, only the trial arm and the shaft form the single plane. The lead arm serves totally different functions in the setup and the swing. These functions are to obtain the leverage and to extend the club head to its fullest to create club head speed as it moves around the pivot point, the lead shoulder. As stated before the lead shoulder is the pivot point in the swing. Leverage and extension are what produce the power in the swing. This is why maintaining spine angle is so important, (see Spinal Alignment). The steadier the spine angle, the more consistent the pivot point. The more consistent the pivot point, the more consistent the swing will be which will lead to a more consistent ball strike. The more the consistent the ball strike, the lower your scores will be.

Chapter 6

SINGLE PLANE SETUP

Driver   7 Iron

Driver   7 Iron

Setup is the most important fundamental but the most overlooked and the least practiced. The reason for this is simply human nature. We as humans always try to find the easiest and quickest way to do anything. Golf is no exception. The average golfer tries to play before they learn how to swing. Then they try to learn the golf swing before they learn how to get a good setup. This is the opposite of what they should do and as someone said a long time ago, that's putting the cart in front of the horse. Take a look at and let me explain the setup when it comes to the single plane swing, but first we must understand the Four Fundamentals of the Single Plane Swing, they are;

#1 the single plane, because when created by the set up and maintained throughout the swing, it allows the golfer to consistently return the club head back to the ball. Chapter 5

#2 a stable stance, because it will help the golfer maintain good balance and posture in order to control the single plane movement. Chapter 6

#3 facing the ball at impact, because it will allow the golfer to swing down the target line more consistently and create a longer Square Tracking motion in the swing. Chapter 7

#4 is the trail hand palm grip, which allows the golfer to return the clubface back to square throughout the impact zone. Chapter 6

As stated before, You don't need to know how to play golf in order to learn a good setup! But you will need to learn a good set-up, "TO PLAY GOOD GOLF"!

I know of no one that would try to build a house on a cracked or shaky foundation. This is what happens when someone tries to make a golf swing without having a good foundation (the setup). Just as building a home on a shaky foundation the golf swing without the good setup will be inconsistent and will not last. Will the setup be the same for everyone? NO. The fundamentals of the setup will be the same, but just as everybody is different, so are the setups. I will say that everyone should try to get as close as they can to what is explained in this chapter.

Getting a good setup makes the golf swing so much easier because it allows the body to repeat the same motion every time. If you can make the same movement every time it makes it a lot easier to learn that movement, but if you try to learn that same movement from different positions it makes it that much harder. Anytime there's a difference in your setup, no matter how small, the body has to adjust to that difference just to try and make the same swing.

It had been said and I agree with that 80% of shot making can be contributed to setup alone. Just think if you can stop 80% of the flaws in your swing before you even swing a club isn't it worth learning? When learning a setup, it is a lot easier when you work from your feet up, not from your head down. What is meant by this is the feet are flat to the ground from heel to toe and 90 degrees from your intended line of target.

"NOTE" when learning the setup it is easier to learn from the feet up but when performing a single plane swing it must be from the shoulders down. In other words, you learn from the feet up but swing from the shoulders down!

First the feet, the feet should be flat to the ground and square to the target line. Stand with your feet together and this will put your feet square to the line as long as your toes of both your feet are on that target line. It's important to note that when you move your feet from this position you move your feet straight on the target line keeping them square to that line. Your feet should feel solid to the ground but they do not have roots. In other words they are flat to the ground but they still have to work.

Stable Stance

What is meant by stable stance? It has been said that in a single plane setup you need to have a wide stance. Although it is true that the stance is wider than in conventional golf, you can get your feet too wide. If your feet are too close together in your setup, you will have a tendency to swing from your legs up, activating the hips and swinging from over the top, (outside to inside the target line). If your feet are too wide, although you will be stable, it will not allow you to finish your swing to a good high balance finish and then you will put strain on your lower back. So what is a stable stance? The answer is: the inside width of the feet should be the width of the outside of your shoulders. We can make sure that we get the right stance by simply knowing something about your body. When your feet are together instep-to-instep, the outside width of the feet is half the width of your shoulders and your feet are in a square position. If this is hard to believe, put your feet together and have somebody measure them and compare it to your shoulders. With your feet together and your toes on the target line, place a golf ball between your feet. Step straight to the side <u>with the lead foot</u> the width of your lead foot times two, now the inside your feet will be half the width of your shoulders, move your trail foot straight to that side the width of your foot times two. At this point your feet are the width of your shoulders and you should fell weight on the arches of your feet. If your feet are too narrow you will feel weight on the top of your foot, and if the feet are wider than your shoulders, you with feel the weight on the ankles. The ball position is now directly in the middle of your stance. This ball position is now where you want it with your shortest five clubs, 9-iron through lob wedge. Now not only have you learned how to get a stable stance we also learned how to get the correct ball position from front to rear. It is important that you maintain this ball position in regards to the lead put with all clubs no <u>matter what you're hitting off the ground</u>. Only the distance between your trail foot and the ball will change depending on length of the clubs shaft. The statement above is so important that I will repeat it <u>"ball position in regard to the lead foot should not change with any club as long as it is being hit off the ground"</u>.

NOTE: *the above stable stance is just a starting point in your correct setup. Will it be the same for every golfer? No! After you have learned the complete setup, you will have to tweak it to fit your body and/or swing.*

Some things to keep in mind when tweaking the stance is if it is too narrow, you will have the tendency to put too much hip turn in the forward swing making a pull shot or a fade to slice. If it is too wide you may not get the right shoulder turn in the back swing making your swing to be out of time. Also, you will not get the complete finish to the lead side which can cause a blocked shot or a loss in power and <u>a sore lower back</u>.

Balance and Posture

Balance

Balance is synonymous with posture but posture is not synonymous with balance. What this means is - you cannot be in balance and be out of posture but you <u>can</u> be in posture and out of balance. Let's explore and find out what is meant by this. Balance in the setup and balance at impact is different.

It is worth saying that balance is a five part procedure that starts with setup. These five are:

#1 address position.

#2 top of the back swing.

#3 through the impact zone.

#4 finish of the swing.

#5 your mind.

#1 the address position......80% on heels, 20% on the balls of the feet.

When getting your balance and Posture you will notice that the tip of your rear is the same distant away from your heels as your nose is away from your toes. also your shoulders are over your toes and your kneecaps is over your shoes laces! As seen in the picture above.

As stated, the weight in <u>a good balanced setup</u> should have 80% of the weight on the heels with 20 percent of the weight on the balls of the feet at address. To understand the before statement you must first understand the dynamics of a golf swing. A good way to think of this is remembering when you were young and tied a string to a rock then swung it around you. The faster you swing the rock, the tighter the string got; it's the same thing with a golf club. When swinging a golf club around your body, the head of the club is moving in an orbit, just like that rock, and just like the rock the faster you swing the club in that orbit, the heavier it will get in what is known as inertia weight or "centrifugal force". The approximate weight of the head of a golf club is 1 ½ lb of dead weight. When the club head is moving around the body at 100 mph the head of the golf club will go from 1 1/2 lb. of dead weight to 65 lb of inertia weight pulling away from your body through the impact zone. To counteract this inertia weight pulling away from your body, one must setup with the weight 80 percent on the heels to allow the swing to pull you into the arches of the feet through the impact zone, where we need it in the #3 balance position.

#2 is at the top of the back swing.......80% heels 20% balls of the feet.

At the top of the backswing position, the balance should still be the same as at setup - 80% heels 20% balls of feet.

#3 Balances though the Impact Zone............
In the arches of the feet.

Let me start by saying that this stage of balance, (impact zone) is the only position that matters when it comes to impacting the ball. Unfortunately, this balance position is almost impossible to achieve without the preceding two being accomplished correctly.

As stated above, balance in the setup and balance at impact is different. Let me explain - maintaining balance throughout the impact zone is to have the weight in the arches of the feet at moment of impact.

If your balance point or weight is in the arches of your feet at setup, the motion of the swing - with the inertia weight of the club - will pull the weight or center of gravity off from the arches on to the toes at moment of impact. But if the majority of the weight, 80% is on the heels of your feet then the inertia of the club builds up and pulls your body forward toward the arches at impact where you need it.

A good way to check this out is to get your normal set up and just move your arms away from you until a club head is about 2 in. off the ground. Maintaining your balance and posture, have someone pull the club towards the ground away from the body and see where your weight goes. If your weight moves toward the balls of your feet then obviously the weight is too far forward at address. Practice getting your setup with your weight 80 percent on the heels and 20 percent on the balls of your feet and then try the same exercise and see if the weight does not go to the arches.

#4 the complete finish position of the swing.

From heel to toe outside the lead foot and on the toe of the trail foot with the sole of that foot facing away from the target.

#5 Balance in your mind

Again, a good way to check this out is to get your normal set up and just move your arms away from you until a club head is about 2 in. off the ground. Maintaining your balance and posture have someone pull the club towards the ground away from the body and see where your weight goes. Next thing is to make sure to stay in your balance and posture, then close your eyes and think of the weight going to your toes, don't move, just think about it. While in the position, have someone to pull the club towards the ground away from the body and see where your weight goes. You will be surprised to find that although you have not moved, the center of you weight will have moved to your toes - because of your mind. So as you can see, you have to think you are in balance - as well as feel you are.

Posture

As stated before, the good balanced setup starts with the stable stance and moves up. Once your feet establish a good stable stance and understand balance we must now put the emphasis on posture. The next step in achieving good posture is knee flex.

What is knee flex and how to get it and why? Knee flex is no more than your knees relaxed out of joint. This can best be described by locking your knee joints in position and then relaxing them out of joint. With this the weight of your body will be supported by bone. Bone is rigid and will always come back to the exact same spot. If you have more of a knee flex your body will be supported by muscle in the legs and must receive the signal from the brain to return back to the original position. If the knee flex is correct in your setup the muscles in the thighs will be soft and pliable in a relaxed position. If you bend your knees too much and have too much knee flex, the muscles in your thighs will be taught and in a rigid position. As stated in grip pressure, the muscles of your body should be in a relaxed position in order to produce power in the golf swing. A muscle in a rigid position resists movement and although you will have a sensation of strength, it will reduce the flexibility in movement of that muscle therefore putting it in a weak position.

Next take a club and hold it across your midsection. While keeping the knees in the flex position and the club across your midsection gently nudge the club backward while letting your shoulders come in a downward move until almost all of the weight is on the heels of your feet. When doing this - the upper body must stay in alignment with the spinal column as it moves. This means from your tailbone through your head. While in this position allow your body (in one solid unit) to pivot forward toward your toes until you get 20 percent of your body weight on the balls of your feet. At this point your shoulders should be directly over your toes; your knees will be over your shoelaces. The outside of your rear will be as far behind your heels and as far as your nose is in front of your toes. At this time you may discover a little discomfort in your lower back. This is to be expected because you have nothing in front of you to counterbalance your rear. At this point - hold your club and get into a single plane, with your arms extended in front of you in a single plane lower your arms from your shoulders to where the sole of the club is flat on the ground, maintaining the single plane. You may notice at this time the tension in the lower back has gone away. This is because the arms and the club are extended past your body to the ball position and counterbalanced the weight of your rear. By this time your body should be in a relaxed and comfortable position, one that you can stand in for extended time to allow yourself to practice.

Spinal Alignment

Setup From the trail side Impact

Setup From the front Impact

Next, we move to your upper body, we start with spinal alignment. As stated above, spinal alignment is best described as the angle in which your spine is in line from your tailbone through the head, through the head, through the head. Have I made this clear? In every swing, there is a certain amount of spinal tilt away from the target and so it is in a single plane swing. Note, when getting in the posture, don't let your head drop out of alignment with your spinal column. The reason there is more spinal tilt in the single plane setup and swing is because your arms are the same length. With the arms being the same length and with the trail hand grip below the lead hand some 3" to 4". What this means is the trail shoulder will be lower than the lead in order to set the spine angle at address and to keep the arms straight.

Because there is more spine tilt in the single plane setup than in the traditional setup, (because the grip/hold) you will need to practice a couple drills to make sure it becomes natural to you.

The first drill you can do is, making sure you are in a good balanced posture get your grip/hold on the golf club and extend your arms straight out in front of you making sure the lead arm and shaft are in line with each other. While in that good balanced and posture, lower your arms from the shoulders until the head of the club touches the ground. At this time you will notice your trail shoulder is lower than the lead side and the arms form the letter "y".

The second drill is, while in a good balanced posture, extend only the lead arm out in front of you making sure the shaft in the arm is in a straight line and simply lower it to the ground. Next, take the trail palm of your hand and place it on the side of the trail leg. Next, move your palm down your leg until it is right above the knee and the trail arm is straight. From this position, reach up from underneath the club and place your trail hand below the lead hand making sure they touch. After you have the correct hold on the club, make sure the lines of straight and you still remain your posture. At this time you will also notice, as in the first drill - that the trail shoulder is lower than the lead shoulder and the arms and club form the letter "y". Now you can understand what is meant by the "y" angle and why it's so important.

This is the biggest flaw that most golfers will allow to happen. Remember, when it comes to swinging a golf club, up and down, back-and-forth, side to side has nothing to do with parallel to the ground but has everything to do with spine angle. Just as your spinal angle is on an angle other than parallel, so will the angles of the golf swing. The main reason most senior golfers lower their heads at address is because of their bi-focal glasses. A golfer that has bi-focal glasses on while playing golf will have a tendency to drop their head at address to see over top of the bi-focals therefore putting their head out of position.

To understand this one must know why and how to get these angles properly. But first we must understand why we need a trail hand palm grip/hold.

The golf grip/hold is one of the most important aspects of the game of golf. It is the only thing that connects the human body to the golf club. Therefore it is very important that we have the proper grip for the swing we are trying to achieve. The grip/hold will be explained in this chapter.

I am convinced that not all one grip is suitable to everyone. Just like there are different types of body structures, flexibility, heights and weights, there are different grips that best relate to these different types.

The grip must allow the golfer to accomplish certain things during the swing. These things are:

#1 allow the golfer to get into a single plane.

#2 allow the blade of the club to come back to square to the line moving down that line, refer back to chapter on impact zone.

#3 allow the golfer to achieve a full wrist cock at the top of his backswing.

#4 must not be responsible for an early release of the wrists and hands before impact. In other words the grip shall allow the hands to lead the club through impact.

#5 must be free enough to allow the golfer to complete the swing.

The grip that is chosen may be an overlapping grip, the interlocking grip, the ten-finger grip or a single plane trail hand palm grip. It has been my experience that the single plane trail hand palm grip is the best grip for most of my students, about 95%. I am convinced that the single plane is easier to get and maintain using the palm grip in the trail hand. Therefore, it should be the grip for most people and the grip that is taught by instructors when teaching the single plane swing.

It is worth noting that I have found that when a golfer is trying to learn a new grip, they will have a tendency to regrip during the swing. In other words, the golfer will have a tendency to grip tighter at the top of their backswing than they did in their address. This regriping of the club in most cases we'll close the blade of the club at moment of impact causing the ball to draw or hook. With this in mind, choose the proper grip that will allow you to release the club in time through the ball at impact while remaining in the correct plane.

The grip the golfer chooses must allow for the arms and club to reach full extension at the #4 timing position. In my own experimentation I have found that the reach of my arms are not equal. The reach of my lead arm is 1 1/2 inches longer than my trail arm. This can make as much as 10 of 15 yards difference with the exact same swing depending on the individual and body type. In my particular case using the single plain palm grip my 5 iron went 172 yd. on average but when it 192 yds with the overlapping palm grip. A difference of 20 yd. with the exact same swing just a different grip setup. What I have found is with the reach of my right arm being shorter than my left, it made for an early release of the golf club through impact. I also got what is called golfers elbow. This was because of trying to swing to the #4 timing position made me hyperextend my right elbow. Therefore, I come to the conclusion that the most important thing in the single plane swing is not the traditional single plane rear hand palm grip, but rather how we adapt the rear hand palm grip to the individual student. With this being said, I have always come to the conclusion that it's not the position of the rear hand up and down the handle so much as it is the rotation of the rear hand in the setup which will allow the golfer to get into a single plane and help maintain it throughout the swing.

Again, as I stated previously in this book, there are four basic fundamentals and the single plane set up in swing which are single plane, stable stance, place a ball of impact, and trail hand palm grip. If I had to rate the single plane four fundamentals in order of importance I believe they are:

#1 the single plane, created by the set up and maintain through to swing, see chapter 4.

#2 is a stable stance, because it will help the golfer to maintain a good balance and posture in order to stay in the single plane. See chapter 4.

#3 is facing the ball at impact, because it will allow the golfer to more consistently swing down the target line.

#4 is the trail hand palm hold - grip. See chapter 4.

Holding the Club

When getting the palm grip for a single plane swing. it's important to note that only the trail hand is in the palm, the lead hand is quite similar to the conventional grip except at address the lead wrist it is in an uncocked position, the handle only goes in the palm of the trail hand, <u>not in the lead hand.</u> The rotation and placement of the trail hand with the uncocking of the lead wrist at address is the grip that is necessary to achieve a single plane setup.

Now let us take a closer look at each hand and explain these in detail. First we shall start with the lead hand. Hold the your lead hand in front of you with your palm facing you, cup your hand and looking at it you will see that there will be two lines that run across your hand. These lines or what's known as the golfer's lines. Place the grip between the golfer's lines of your lead hand and the first crease between the knuckle and the first joint of your index finger. With the toe the club pointed up and the back of your hand pointed toward the target, raise your thumb straight up. With the club in this location in your lead hand close only the fingers around the grip. Hold the club directly in front of your body and relaxed your wrist until the club points away from you, only at this point do you lower your thumb on to the shaft. You will notice that the shaft of the club and your arm is on a straight line and the shaft of the club will not be on plain with the lead arm but will be in a parallel line directly below the lead arm. Note also, when the lead hand is in the proper grip the back of the lead hand and the blade of the club will both be in line with the target.

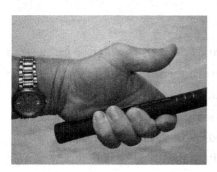 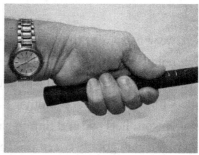

The lead wrist will be in an uncocked position and resemble the position you will be at in the impact position. When the club and your hand is in the correct position you can hold the club out in front of you and left your thumb and the small 3 fingers away from the club and the club will stay in place. This shows that the grip is underneath the heel pad of your lead hand and in the correct placement of the grip. If the grip of the club is not in the lead hand as described the club will fall out of your hand. If it is in that position during your swing it will be very difficult to allow the club to work as the club was designed.

Now let me explain where the lead hand goes on the handle in its rotation. First thing you need to do is; get the hold as explained above. Second, hook the club onto something like the golf cart making sure the toe is pointing up. Next, pull the club away and using only the shoulder and see where the toe rotates. The club will rotate into its neutral position. If the toe is not pointing straight up in its neutral position, then adjust it in your hand and repeat the above until it does. This it the position your club should be in at address! See - using the black dots in the chapter on drills.

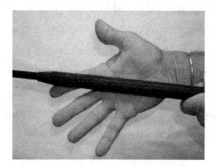 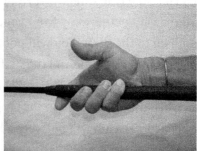

Next, we will examine the trail hand and how important it is to get the trail hand hold correctly. Just as you did with the lead hand look at the palm of your trail hand, there you will notice the same golfer's lines. Above the golfers lines you will see another line right in the middle of your palm between your heel pad and thumb pad. This is known as your lifeline. The grip of the club goes between the golfer's lines and your lifeline, through the middle of the heel pad of your trail hand.

Extend your trail hand out in front of you with your thumb straight up. The fingers should be slightly separated. Rotate your hand so that your thumb is 45 degrees toward to trail side.

Place the club in the palm as described. Start by closing your smallest finger first then the next and the next until all fingers are gripping the club. At this time the thumb is pointing up. The thumb is the last to go on the club. It will go on and direct line of your forearm. You will notice that the palm of your hand appears to be pointed up away from the ground, but actually the power point of your hand, which is directly under your thumb, is pointed at the target, not up. To prove this, hold your thumb in place and open your fingers and palm to its fullest extent. Now you will notice that the palm your hand is facing the target not up. This is an optical illusion because when you get the hold with trail hand you're wrapping your fingers around the handle not your thumb. See drill on grip/hold, using the black dots.

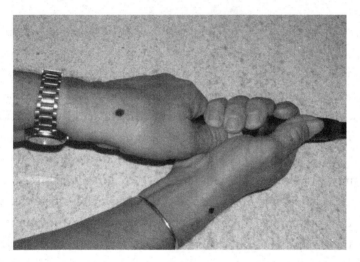

The wrist of your trail arm should be straight and in a neutral position. In other words, your hand, wrist and forearm should be straight with each other. When you have the correct grip and your hand and arm are in the correct position, the end of the grip at address will be pointing to your lead shoulder not up the trail arm. If the end of the grip is pointed at your body or up the trail arm at address, then your wrist has a bow in them. If you have a bow in the wrist at setup - you will have the tendency to release the club too early in the forward swing.

Remember the wrist of your trail arm must be in a neutral position at address. To best illustrate this, get a hammer and pretend to drive a nail into a board on a table. Next, pretend to drive a nail into a wall on the lead side. You may note that you did not rotate the hammer in your hands to nail that nail into a wall but simply rotated the hammer and your hand and wrist to accommodate a straight-line motion. To use a hammer affectively you will always use a hammer in a straight-line motion no matter where you will be using it. If you hammer a nail into a board on the table, the hammer will come straight up and down without you even thinking about it. If you nail a nail into a wall or the ceiling the hammer will come away from that nail in a straight line without thinking about it. This is why in the early days the single plane golf swing was known as the straight-line motion swing. I know of no one that will turn or rotate the hammer in his or her hand to nail a nail. Notice the position of the trail wrist and hand when pretending to nail that nail into that wall. Your wrist and arm are in a straight neutral position and your hands are in exact position mentioned above.

What is this position? Simply put, this is the most athletic and powerful position your arm can be in. In this position your hand and arm and work in a straight-line motion (single plane) without restriction. So if you ever want to know where your hand should be just pick up a hammer and drive some nails into a wall. This is why the single plane swing is described in the trail hand grip as the hammer effect.

Grip Pressure

There seems to be a lot of confusion about grip pressure, how to get the correct grip pressure and how to maintain the correct grip pressure throughout the swing. Mr. Norman said he felt like he was ringing a chicken's neck with his grip pressure is his lead hand. This gave the wrong impression of what his grip pressure really was. Yes, He felt that way but, Mr. Norman was left-handed swinging his clubs right handed! That is why he felt that way. I asked him on one of the Natural Golf certified instructor's clinics he gave if I could feel his forearms when he was at address and to my shock he said yes! At address when he said he had a tight grip pressure, his forearms were relaxed. No one can have tight grip pressure with relaxed forearms. If a golfer swings from their opposite, the subservient side, they will be using the opposite side of their brain. This will lead to different feeling than ours that swings from their dominate side.

Let's start out by saying grip pressure in itself is very small. With that said, I have the sensation at address that my trail hand is locked in position more than my lead hand but without any tension, as stated before tension is a killer. I did not have that sensation with the conventional swing because of the shape of the handle. That sensation in my trail hand also helps me stay on plane better.

The tighter you grip the club, the less the club can work as the engineer designed the club to work. It has been said by some teachers that, "you hold the club in your hand like you would hold a bird, if you hold the bird to tight you will kill it, if you hold it too loosely it will fly away". The question I have is," are you holding a baby chick or are you holding an eagle?" These are both birds but you have to hold them very differently. Some say it's like holding a pistol, too tight and you pull it off target, too loose and it falls out of your hand. Now the same question, "are you holding a 22 target pistol or are you holding a 44 Magnum", both are pistols but you also hold them very differently. Perception! If I ask you to think of the color red which color red are you thinking of? If there were ten of us thinking of the color red, all would probably be thinking of a different color red, but they all would be red, perception! With this in mind I describe grip pressure this way: at one time in our life we all have had a child ask us to arm-wrestle. So now we put our arm on the table and the child grabs hold of our hand and tries to pull our arm down. We don't try to put the child's hand down, we let him or her pull on our arm and it does not move, this is grip pressure and this is how we get it. First, put your hands on the grip and wrap your fingers around it, now lock your fingers in place with as little pressure as possible, just enough so you can pick up your club but do not squeeze the grip. Both hands should have the same amount of pressure on the grip at address and throughout the swing. A good way to check this is to always have loose forearms (relaxed forearms) when applying your grip at address. This is all the grip pressure you will ever need to swing a golf club. Have you ever seen a set of Chinese handcuffs? If you put your fingers in the handcuffs and then try to pull your fingers out, the more you try to pull your fingers out the more your fingers get bonded to the handcuffs. This is what happens in your golf grip. The faster you swing the club the more your fingers gets bonded to the club without you squeezing.

Let me explain, the head of the golf club weighs about a pound and a half (dead weight). The faster you swing the club, the more inertia weight is generated by that pound and a half. The faster you swing the club the more the inertia weight pulls away from your body and the more your hands bound together on the golf club, just like with the Chinese handcuffs. The inertia weight will apply all the necessary grip pressure you will ever need in your swing. With this in mind just lock your fingers around the club and swing.

Remember you cannot swing a golf club in a flex position; you have to be comfortable and relaxed. If your grip is too tight it will build tension in your forearms (this is what is meant by a flexed position) then to your upper arms, then to your back, and then to your complete body. A good demonstration of this is, hold your arm out straight to your side and make a fist, now flex your fist and bend your arm. This is like swinging a golf club with tight grip pressure. Now hold your arm out to your side and relax your hand and bend your arm. Feel how free and easy it moves. This is like swinging a golf club in a relaxed position, and this is what we're trying to achieve with the right grip pressure. Remember just arm wrestle that child. With that being said, I have found that when making less than full swing or when hitting a wedge I like to have the sensation of a little more trail hand pressure than lead hand just to control my plane, not too much as to interfere with the swing.

Another aspect of grip pressure has to do with the club design itself. Each set of clubs have thousands of dollars and hundreds of hours of research and development in its design. The head of the club is engineered to perform in a certain way under normal conditions. Since we were born, we have tried to manipulate everything that we do. You cannot manipulate a golf swing; you just have to let it work. When you grip a golf club too tight, you in effect are trying to manipulate the golf club instead of letting the club work the way it was designed to work. In other words, the tighter you grip the club, the less value of a club becomes.

Ball Position

One of the most frequently asked questions I get from single plane swing golfers is about ball position. "Where is the correct ball position and how can I make sure I get it right every time?" This is a very good question, but the answer is simple if you don't overthink it.

I have found that students can learn in many ways. People are not the same so it stands to reason that they learn differently. Some can learn by watching, some by doing and some have to have the smallest thing explained in detail. I have, I think, come up with the two best ways to explain why and where ball position is where it is. Both will work. Only you know how you learn, so try the first way and if it doesn't work try the second; please don't try to combine the two.

Ball position first of all requires a correct setup. Only after all the steps in the setup chapter have been taken can we properly discuss ball position. In the setup chapter, we discussed ball position relative to the lead foot; now let's explore the remaining details of ball position.

It will help if we are all on the same page when it comes to the nomenclature of ball position. See the picture below; which applies to a right-handed golfer; for lefties it's the reverse.

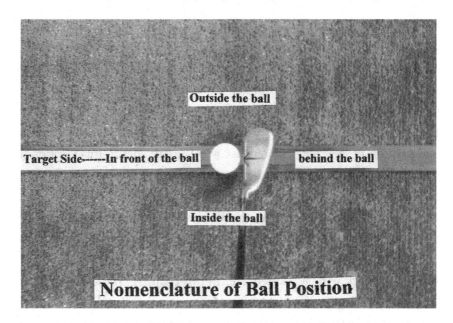

Nomenclature of Ball Position

What is meant by ball position is where the ball is placed on the ground that will put it in the way of the swing. This can be done "two" ways; the 1st way is in the single plain swing is to know that all pall position is the correlation of two radii's as explained below. The 2nd way will be explained later in this chapter.

In other words, how far you stand from the ball and where the ball is on the ground from left to right with any given club is ball position. The important factor of ball position is **not** where the ball is at address but rather where the ball will be at **moment of impact**. Ball position front to rear at moment of impact should be approximately 1 ½" to 2" behind the lead shoulder. Knowing this we must adjust our address ball position to make the impact ball position proper. Some golfers ask why the ball goes in this position. I answer this way. It is because the forward shoulder is the pivot point in your swing. What this means is your forward shoulder, hand and club form a straight line at address. This puts the bottom of your swing arc under your forward shoulder and in front of your ball position to insure you swing with a descending arc and acceleration through the ball (with all clubs except the driver which will be covered later in this chapter). The shoulders and breastbone are fixed and will not move closer or further away in relationship to each other. So therefore the ball position does not change in relationship to the forward foot with any club, (except the driver). This also explains why your head is over your rear knee at address and stays there throughout the swing. If your head moves from side to side during your swing, your shoulder will move from side to side, and it in turn will move the bottom of your arc forward. When this happen you may de-loft your club or top the ball and the ball will go low depending where your head moved to out of position at impact. In short the ball flight may go anywhere!

Ball position may vary a small amount with each golfer, but it is important that it remains constant with that golfer and with every swing as long as the ball is being hit on the ground! The best way to achieve this is PRACTICE! PRACTICE! PRACTICE!

I say this because not all golfers have the same posture, body style or flexibility. I believe it would be very beneficial for all golfers to start their ball position from left to right or forward to rear in the middle of their stance with the shortage clubs and simply tweak it to accommodate their body style. After they have tweaked their ball position, that position relative to the lead foot should never change as long as the ball is being hit on the ground. Reason for this in a single plane swing the golfer swings around the lead shoulder not your sternum. This makes the middle of you swing your lead shoulder not your sternum. With this being so the bottom of the arc of the swing will be directly under the lead shoulder. **The shoulder position should not change with any club or swing.** We always try to impact a ball on the descending arc of the swing when hitting the ball on the ground. Therefore the ball should always be 1 1/2 to 2 in. behind the bottom of the arc of that swing, the lead shoulder. Find this position through experimentation and keep it always. Try to never let it move. You may want to draw a diagram of your ball position with regards to the lead foot and put it in your golf bag for future reference. Your memory may fade but the writing of your notes will always be the same. Although the ball position will seem to move forward when your feet get wider, it will stay the same in relationship to the forward foot. With the shortest shafted clubs, the inside of your feet should be shoulder width and with the longer shafted club (driver), the inside of your feet should be shoulder width plus one-foot width. This is done to maintain balance and control.

With the driver, I teach the golfer that they should step to the side with the forward foot one-foot width. This is done so you do not have to change your swing to hit the driver and you can still hit the driver on the flat part of the swing. In other words, you need to have the bottom of your swing arc at or just behind your ball so the ball will be contacted at the flat part of the swing or on a slightly upward path when swinging a driver. Again, the forward foot at address does this.

How far do you stand from the ball and why? The first thing you want to do when getting ball position away from you is to review balance and posture. Never get out of balance and posture to get ball position. I cannot emphasize this enough! While standing in a good balance posture and the correct grip, allow the arms to straighten out front of you getting a single plane then lower your arms from the shoulders down towards the ground maintaining that single plane until the club touches the ground. If you raise and lower your arms in this position several times you will notice that the club head is moving in a radius. Remember do not get out of balance and posture. When you let the club head go to the ground on that radius and then across it with the single plane radius in the swing this is ball position. To put it simply ball position is the combination of two radii. When looking at ball position it's almost as if you're looking through a riflescope and the cross hairs on a riflescope and the ball position on the ground can be visualized to be the same. Just remember the cross hairs are 1/2 to 2 in. behind the lowest part of the swing that is directly under your shoulder. I know what I keep writing sounds a little redundant but is that important that you remember it!

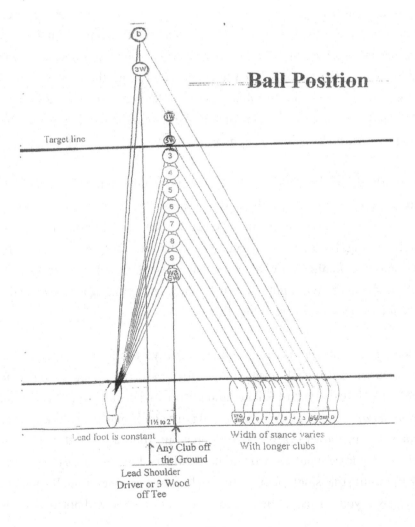

Ball Position

CLUBS MUST BE POSITIONED THE SAME, EVERY TIME. If the toe is off the ground, then the golfer will be standing too far from the ball and the ball will have the tendency to go left. If the heel is off the ground, the golfer will be standing too close to the ball and the ball will have the tendency to go right.

Another question I am asked is, "Why do my feet get wider in my stance with the longer clubs?" Again, the answer is simple. The arc of the swing gets longer with the longer shafts. By that I mean that the head of the club moves further away from, and around your body with the longer shaft. So with the arc becoming longer, you will have a slightly longer weight transfer in your swing. With this slightly longer natural weight transfer, you have to keep your center of gravity (breastbone) between your arches of your feet to maintain balance and control during the transition from the back to forward swing. Therefore, the longer the shafts, the wider your feet, and the wider your feet the more you are stable and can control the wider weight transfer. Remember, for most golfers for the shortest shafted clubs, the inside of your feet should be shoulder width, and with the longer shafted club (the driver), the inside of your feet should be shoulder width plus one foot width at address. Another added benefit from this setup is that your head is behind the ball at address and has a natural tendency to stay there throughout the complete swing. With this ball position (setup), all the golfer has to do is learn one golf swing, and then repeat it every time no matter what club they are using. CHANGE GOLF CLUBS, NOT GOLF SWINGS.

Next get your single plane golf grip/hold with the little finger of your lead hand about one and a half-in. down the grip. Make sure this move is the same with every club, every time. The reasoning behind this is that when a golfer moves there hand up and down the grip for every 1/2" travel the club head can move as much as 2" in that radius.

It is important at this time to explain that the golfer should aim the golf club as he/she would aim a rifle. Most golfers aim their clubs like they would a shotgun. By this, I mean they square their club in the general direction of the target and swing. I teach that the better the aim of the club, the better the chance of hitting the target. The way the irons are aimed is different from the way the woods are aimed. I will talk about the irons first and then about the woods.

With the way the irons are designed with the toe so much larger than the heel so at address the only part of the club that looks straight (or square) to you are the bottom lines on the face of the club. With this in mind, use the bottom lines and align them 90 degrees from the intended line of flight. With the bottom lines at 90 degrees to the intended line of flight, the club is now aimed at (or square to) the target line. One of the biggest problems most golfers have in alignment is they align their body to their target and then try to align the club. To get the right alignment, you align your club to the target first and then you align your body to your club. See drill on alignment.

The woods are aimed by using the top ridgeline of the club. The way the woods are made on the bottom, the golfer's eye will play tricks on them while at address. By using the lines on the face of the woods like that of the irons, there will be a tendency to open the face of the woods at address, thus making the ball go right. So to aim the woods, always use the top ridgeline at 90 degrees from the intended line of flight. If the club is aimed the way it is supposed to be, the shaft of the club will be a true 90 degrees from the intended line of flight.

Ball Position 2

This is the 2nd way of getting into the correct ball position and is more technical. I highly recommend that you as a golfer do one or the other of these setups – don't mix them for it will be counterproductive. With this in mind, let me explain the best way I have found to instruct someone who needs more of a technical way to achieve their setup. I highly recommend you read and be familiar with the Ball Flight Laws in chapter 2 before reading this technical version. This may be a good time to go back and refresh yourself with that chapter, it will make this technical version easier to understand.

The shaft length of the club (any club) will indicate how far to stand from the ball, and this is how it is done. Just as in the first way - the shaft of the club will determine how far to stand from the ball and the ball position in relationship to the forward foot will never changes with any club that you impact off the ground. Although the ball position will seem to move forward when your feet get wider, it will stay the same in relationship to the forward foot.

First, the sole of the club must to be flat on the ground and placed inside the ball with the tip of the toe of the club touching the ball to about 3" from the ball. In my teaching I found that the taller of the golfers are closer to the ball he will stand at address and the shorter of the golfer the further away the ball will be at address. Remember the shoulder is the pivot point of the swing and is further away from the ground with the taller player. Which makes a more of an upright single plane swing versus the shorter golfer with the pivot point being closer to the ground being more of a flat swing while maintaining the same single plane. The reason for this is simply the shaft of the club. With a modern-day shafts, (especially graphite) the club makers has only a certain amount of tolerances to play with in order to produce a first line quality club. Some of these tolerances are the overall length of the shaft along with the flex, torque and the lie angle of that club head along with others we will get into later in this book. If a club maker makes a shaft too long or too short it will lose the properties of that shaft. These properties are torque and flex. When this happened the golfer will not be able to control their distance, trajectory or ball flight consistently. This being so a tall golfer with their shoulder further from the ground will have to stand closer to the ball at address than a shorter golfer with their shoulder closer to the ground.

This is not a constant but a general rule one has to consider when they gets there set-up. This position will change a little with every golfer but will never be less than the tip of the toe of the club touching the ball to the tip being more than 3" from the ball. Fine the position that is right for you and repeat it every time, every swing.

It is important at this time to explain that the golfer should aim the golf club as he/she would aim a rifle. Most golfers aim their clubs like they would a shotgun. By this, I mean they square their club face in the general direction of the target and swing. I teach that the better the aim of the club, the better the chance of hitting the target. The way the irons are aimed is different from the way the woods are aimed. I will talk about the irons first and then about the woods.

The way to aim the irons is by looking at the bottom lines on the face of the club. Have you noticed that when you buy a new set of clubs the bottom two or three lines on the face of the irons is generally painted white? This is done because the club manufacturer knows that by looking at the face of the club it is almost impossible to square it to the target. That is why the club manufacturer gives the golfer and alignment tool on their clubs which is the white lines. Most Irons are designed with the toe much larger than the heel so at address the only part of the iron club that looks straight, (or square) to you are not the complete face of the club but the bottom lines on the face of that club. With this in mind and using the bottom lines align them 90 degrees from the intended line of flight. With the bottom lines at 90 degrees to the intended line of flight, the club is now aimed at (or square to) the target line. One of the biggest problems most golfers have in alignment is they align their body to their target and then try to align the club. To get the right alignment you align your club to the target first and then you align your body to your club. See the Drill on Alignment to Target.

The woods are aimed by using the top ridgeline on the club. The way the woods are made on the bottom, the golfer's eyes will play tricks on them while at address. By using the lines on the face of the woods like that of the irons, there will be a tendency to open the face of the woods at address, thus making the ball go right or slice. So to aim the woods, always use the top ridgeline at 90 degrees from the intended line of flight. If the club is aimed the way it is supposed to be, the shaft of the club will be a true 90 degrees from the intended line of flight.

Using the shaft as a gauge and keeping it square (90 degrees) to the intended line of flight, put your feet together with that line made by the shaft running between your legs as you look down. With your knees straight, standing tall, move into or away from the ball until the tip of the grip touches you and the sole of the club is flat on the ground. Now you are the right distance from the ball with that club. But remember, your knees have to be straight and your body standing tall. Also as said before the sole of the club must be flat (level) to the ground or all the other measurements will be off! NOTE; All CLUBS MUST BE POSITIONED THE SAME, EVERY TIME. If the toe is off the ground, then the golfer will be standing too far from the ball and the ball will have the tendency to go left or hook. If the heel is off the ground, the golfer will be standing too close to the ball and the ball will have the tendency to go right or slice. See Chapter 2, Ball Flight Laws.

With the shortest shafted clubs, L/W to 9 iron - the inside of your feet should be shoulder width and with the longer shafted club (driver), the inside of your feet should be shoulder width plus one-foot width at address. This is done to maintain balance and control. I have found that for most people, their shoulders are twice the width of their feet when their feet are together. To attain approximate shoulder width, using the shaft of the club, still at 90 degrees from your intended line of flight, place it between your feet. Next, step straight to the side with your forward foot two-foot widths. Make sure you always start by stepping sideways with the lead foot first. If the trail foot is moved first all measurements will be off when getting ball position with the longer clubs. This position with the forward foot remains constant with every club except the driver. With the rear foot, step straight to the side two-foot widths. The longer the club the wider you step with your rear foot. This is the right width for the shortest clubs and puts the ball position in the center of your stance. Remember that the longer the shaft, the further you stand from the ball and the wider your feet are apart. With the shorter shafted clubs, the closer you are to the ball and narrower your feet are apart. But the ball position never changes with any club (except the Driver) in relationship with the forward foot.

To further clarify, the forward shoulder is the pivot point in the single plane swing. The shoulders and breastbone are fixed and will not move a relationship to each other in or out. This also explains why you head is over your rear knee at address and should stay there throughout the swing. If your head moves forward in your swing, your shoulder will move forward, and it in turn will move the bottom of your arc of your swing forward. When this happen you will at best de-loft your club with a lower ball flight or maybe even top the ball or even worse - "shank it." At the moment of impact your lead arm, hand and club head should return to its original set-up position to form a straight line from the lead shoulder to the bottom of your swing arc.

With the above paragraph in mind, let me explain why the driver ball position must change and be on the flat part of the arc in the swing. The lead shoulder is the pivot point which means the flat part of the golf swing is directly under the lead shoulder.

I think it's time to explain what is meant by the flat part of the swing? The term flat part of the swing refers to a horizontal line the club moves on at the bottom of the swing arc. All this means is the club head at the bottom of the swing will be traveling on a horizontal line parallel to the ground but not touching it. See Impact Zone in Chapter 3. It is also important to remember that the ball will be teed up which means the club head should not touch the ground during the swing. If it did it would cause a slight deceleration upon impact. Knowing this, the ball position for the driver must change and this is the way to achieve it.

To achieve the correct ball position for the driver step to the side with the lead foot one-foot width and allow the trail foot to widen and get the necessary distance needed, this is done so you do not have to change your swing to hit the driver and you can still hit the driver on the flat part of your swing. In other words, when impacting the ball on the ground, you need to have the bottom of your swing arc in front of your ball so the ball will be contacted on a slightly downward path. The driver on the other hand should never contact the ground and impact the ball on the flat part of the swing. So remember the bottom of the swing arc and therefore the flat part of the swing is directly under your pivot point which is your lead shoulder. This way when swinging the driver with the ball position under the pivot point the ball can be contacted on the flat part of your swing and again the forward foot at address does this.

Most teachers in the past have taught that to contact the ball properly with the driver the golfer should be swinging slightly on the upward path. Although this may help some golfers get the ball airborne better I believe too much distance has been lost with this aspect of ball position without receiving any more control. I teach it's better to have more loft on the driver and contact ball on the flat of the swing. This position produces more power because the club face is still accelerating through impact and not to impact. See power in the golf swing along with the five timing points in chapter 5 and Impact Zone in chapter 2.

If this can be accomplished it will ensure that the club head will be accelerating through impact of the ball for maximum distance and control.

Using the shaft as a gauge and keeping the face square to the intended line of flight, put your feet together with the line made by that shaft running between your heels as you look down. With your knees straight, standing straight and tall, move into or away from the ball until the tip of the grip touches you and the toe of the club is anywhere between touching the ball to 4" inside the line. Now you are the right distance from the ball with that club. But remember, your knees have to be straight and you have to be standing straight up and tall, also the sole of the club must be flat (level) to the ground or all the other measurements will be off!

How will you know how to get the correct measurement from between the club's toe and the ball to start this setup???

This measurement will depend on two things, the first is the length of your arms and the second your overall height. Knowing this we start by using a marking pencil and drawing a line on the face of the club in the middle from top to bottom. Next place a golf ball on the ground. While in a good balance posture and the correct grip, allow the arms to straighten out in front of you getting a single plain. Never get out of balance and posture to get ball position. I cannot emphasize this enough! Now lower your arms from the shoulders down towards the ground maintaining that single plane until the club touches the ground. Remaining in the correct balance, posture and single plane move your body to get the ball in line with the black line on the face on the club.

Next while keeping the black line on the face of the club in line with the golf ball and without moving your feet stand tall. Using the shaft as a gauge, (keeping the face square to the intended line of flight) return your feet together with the line made by that shaft running between your heels. The last thing to do is to bring the club toward you so the tip of the grip touches you and the soul of the club remains flat on the ground. Now you are the right distance from the ball. Measure between the toe of the club and the ball. This is the distance you place a club in the set-up as long as the ball is being hit off the ground - no matter what length of the shaft. You can even hit a driver off the ground with this set-up. When hitting a driver or three wood off of a tee adjustments have to be made. These adjustments are standing further from the ball and moving the ball position forward at address as mentioned above.

Note: a good rule of thumb is, the longer the shaft, the flatter the swing plane, but the only time adjustments have to be made to the above-mentioned measurements is when hitting a driver or three wood off the tee.

But remember when you are getting this measurement, your knees have to be straight and you have to be standing straight up and tall, also as stated before the sole of the club must be flat (level) to the ground or all the other measurements will be off!

Just remember the arc of the swing gets longer with the longer shafts. By that I mean that the head of the club moves further away from, and around your body with the longer shaft and you have to keep your center of gravity (breastbone) between your arches of your feet to maintain balance and control. Therefore, the longer the shaft, the wider your feet, and the wider your feet the more stable your stance. Just remember not to get your feet too wide with any specific club for this will restrict the release of the club and the follow through of the swing. Another added benefit from this setup is that your head is behind the ball at address and has a natural tendency to stay there throughout the complete swing. With this ball position (setup), all the golfer has to do is learning one golf swing, then repeat it every time no matter what club they are using. CHANGE GOLF CLUBS, NOT GOLF SWINGS.

Next get your single plane palm grip with the little finger of your lead hand (left hand for right hand golfers, right hand for left-hand golfers) about 1" down the handle, make sure this move is the same with very club, every time.

Thereare several things of general information that should be stressed. They are:

1ST. These measurements are for most shots on level ground. Adjustments may need to be made on uneven lies.

2ND. Placement and movements should be rehearsed so much that you do not have to think about them just line up your shot and swing.

3RD. The last movement you have to make is to get into the correct balance and posture, then moves the face of the club from inside the ball to behind the ball.

This will put your hands in a good natural golf, single axis position. Now the golfer knows "where the correct ball position is and how they can make sure they get right every time.

In summary, ball position may vary a small amount with each golfer, but it is important that it remains constant with that golfer and with every swing! The best way to achieve this is, PRACTICE! PRACTICE! PRACTICE! Then go out and enjoy yourself in this beloved game of golf.

THE SINGLE PLANE
GOLF SWING

Just as golf clubs have evolved throughout the years, so as the single plane swing. From the first Scottish sailor who picked up a stick on the beach and swigging it like an axe in order to hit rocks on the beach to Old Tom Morris, who used it to win the British Open, on to Mr. Moe Norman, who perfected it and became the best ball striker in the history of golf.

Mr. Norman reinvented the single plane swing through years of trial and error. He found that after years of practice and hitting millions of golf balls on the practice range that if he rotated the lead hand so that the back of the hand faced the target, he could control the ball flight. He also knew that with the single plane swing he could return a club face back to the ball more consistently and with his new grip he invented, he could make the ball fly perfectly straight. He also knew that if he held the club in the fingers in the trail hand, he would go into the conventional golf setup and that was totally unacceptable to him, so he placed it into the palm. With the grip he invented, he was able to use the trail hand for power, (like swinging a hammer) while the lead hand position directed the ball flight.

I have been told when I demonstrate the swing that the two swings look alike. I answer this way, if they look alike to you then you are not watching the swing, but rather you are watching ball flight. If you will look closely at the swing you will see two very different motions. The conventional swing is a motion where you swing from the feet up while in the single plane swing you swing from the shoulders down.

Throughout history there has only been two occasions when the golf grip evolved in giant leaps. The first of these was when Mr. Harry Varnon invented the overlapping grip and the second when Mr. Moe Norman invented the true single plane golf grip. The conventional golfer can thank Mr. Harry Varnon for the traditional overlapping golf grip while a single plane golfer can thank Mr. Moe Norman. As I have said previously in this book, this is what I think makes him a genius. When all others around him are laughing at this funny looking set up and swing, he ignored them and continued knocking down pins.

The first time I saw Mr. Norman's swing was in Orlando, Florida in 1997. On the driving range, there were several target greens on the driving range. One of these target greens were 230 yards away. Natural Golf at the time had just introduced the beryllium copper fairway woods. Mr. Norman was given a 15° three wood and asked to hit it. He took the club and hit it for the first time approximately 24 times, every one of the balls landed on the green with two of them hitting the pin and one hitting the flag itself. If I ever had any doubts about his ball striking, it was ended - that day. That was the day my job stopped and my passion began. With that, I humbly give you the single plane golf swing as I see it.

See single plane golf grip and chapter 4 and using the black dots in chapter 19.

I know I keep saying the same things but, that's how imported they are, so;

Again I will repeat two very important points, they are - You don't need to know how to play golf in order to learn a good setup! But you will need to learn a good set-up, "TO PLAY GOOD GOLF"!

And,

In the single plane swing there are four basic fundamentals. These four fundamentals are: single plane, stable stance, face the ball at impact and trail hand palm grip. If I had to rate the four fundamentals in order of importance, I believe they are:

#1 the single plane, because when created by the set up and maintained throughout the swing, it allows the golfer to consistently return the club head back to the ball. Chapter 5

#2 a stable stance, because it will help the golfer maintain good balance and posture in order to control the single plane movement. Chapter 6

#3 facing the ball at impact, because it will allow the golfer to swing down the target line more consistently and create a longer Square Tracking motion in the swing. Chapter 7

#4 is the trail hand palm grip, which allows the golfer to return the clubface back to square throughout the impact zone. Chapter 6

The Arms in the Forward Swing

The Sequence of the Swing

The way to hit long consistent shots at the target takes three things. These three things are: angles, leverage, and timing. In this chapter, we will be talking about how to make the single plane swing – starting with the sequence, then tempo & rhythm, followed by power. In the power section, we will explain what and why the core of the swing is so important. I will also explain leverage and finally timing in the swing.

In order to maintain a good swing, it is required that the movements of body be consistent and in sequence. If this is not achieved, then the swing will not consistently maintain the correct angles in right positions to produce the timing in the swing needed to produce the power we are all looking for.

In order to obtain the correct timing, the swing should be started in sequence with a shoulder movement in both the takeaway and forward swing.

Remember: in the setup, the wrist, forearm and hand of the lead side must be straight from the shoulder to the club head and in a neutral position.

What is meant by the correct sequence? The answer is - because in the single plane swing we swing from the shoulders down, the shoulders will always lead. The proper swing sequence, therefore, is this: in the backswing, the shoulders move first to produce the one-piece takeaway, the arms will start their movement at this time and will in turn move to the body to #2 timing position.

The same can be said for the forward swing. The shoulders will move the arms from the top of the back swing to the #3 timing position. Only after the #3 position has been achieved will the arms start their forward extending movement.

With this being so, the sequence of the swing is- shoulders – arms, shoulders – arms! This will be explained further later in this chapter.

This sequence in the single plane swing has changed slightly as it has evolved, and here is why. In a clinic, Mr. Norman was asked why his club head was so far away from the ball at address. His answer was that by doing so, all he needed to do to start his backswing was to bend his trail arm. When Mr. Norman learned the swing, he addressed the ball with his hands in the middle of his stance. He also had a straight angle with his lead arm and club shaft that meant that his club head was in his setup anywhere from 2" to 14"behind the ball. So with his setup and always keeping his hands body-centered, the club head was positioned progressively farther away from the ball as the length of shaft increased. For example, when he was using a wedge, his club head was some2"away from the ball at address but conversely with a driver – the shaft being much longer - the club head was about 12 to 14" behind the ball.

This led to a lot of confusion with some of our students. Some felt they had to place the club head the exact same distance from the ball at address as Mr. Norman did. This measurement could only have been the same if they were the same size and body type as Mr. Norman – a 220 pound 5 ft.7 in. man with long arms!

Natural Golf's advisory committee set out to find a way to explain these setups so that they could be understood better. What we came up with is this. Center the club head to your body, not the hands. This little change in the setup made a big change in teaching the swing. Although this simplifying of the address position made it easier to understand the setup, it added an extra move in the backswing sequence. With this new address position, it is necessary to rotate the shoulders slightly to get to the same position as Mr. Norman did when he started his backswing. This move is better known as a one-piece takeaway. Mr. Norman didn't need the one-piece takeaway because, with his setup, he was already in position to start the arms.

What we found out was – in the setup position when keeping a straight lead arm - and positioning the hands in the center of the body, it will result in a position of the club head that is farther from the ball than if the club head were body-centered at address.

The best way I can describe the difference in the two sequences because of the different setupsis this. If the hands are body-centered, then there is no need for a one-piece takeaway and the arms can start the swing by bending the trail elbow. Therefore the sequence will be arms, shoulders, arms.

If the club head is body-centered, there must be a one-piece takeaway. The one-piece takeaway adds an additional movement to the sequence. This setup will be started with a shoulder rotation – not by hands or arm movement. Therefore the sequence form this setup will be shoulders, arms, shoulders, arms.

I feel that both setup positions are correct as long as the golfer applies the sequences for the setup they chose. I feel that it's up to the individual golfer to decide which setup and swing sequence they feel more comfortable using.

Again, if the hands are body-centered, it requires that the sequence of swing movements be – arms – shoulders –arms. But if the club head is body-centered it requires that the sequence of that swing movements be shoulders – arms, shoulders – arms!

Tempo

To clarify the difference between tempo and rhythm think of a porch swing. The time it takes a porch swing to make a complete swing is what we call tempo. But how fast the porch swing moves to the rear and forward is what we call rhythm. In order for the golfer to produce a repeating swing, he/she must swing all clubs as close to the same temple and rhythm as possible. All the golf clubs in your bag have different length shafts and this is what makes different club head speeds. Think of it this way, if an airplane was five miles up in the air and went around the world in 24 hours, it would be moving approximately 1,000 miles per hour, right? But if a satellite was in a 25,000 mile orbit and it went around the world in the same 24 hours but in a different orbit it would be moving a lot faster than that of the airplane, right? But the arc that they were on would be moving the same. When it comes to the golf swing you can think of your sand wedge as being the airplane and your driver as being the satellite. They will both be moving the same speed in their rotation but with different club head speeds. So to put it in simple terms; the golf swing increases and decreases its club head speed with the length to the club shaft, not by changing the speed in which it is swung. This can be proven by a radar meter or gage.

Rhythm

Rhythm, on the other hand, can and must be controlled. Rhythm is the speed the golf club travels in the backswing and in the forward swing. Or to put it another way - the speed in which you swing your golf club in time = Rhythm. I will start out by saying that "one hundred percent makes up the sum of any whole". It doesn't matter what the whole is, it may be your shoe, your hat, your car or golf ball, whatever. In a golf swing, that <u>sum</u> is your tempo. This is the part of the swing one must not try to change. All golfers have their own tempo, it's God given - just enjoy. It's just the way you look at things. Think of it this way - If you have a golf ball in your hand, what percent would you have? 100% of a golf ball, right? If you cut that golf ball in half and put each half in separate hands what will you have? 50 percent of the ball in each hand? " No", you have 100 percent of a half golf ball, because now the sum is only a half a ball! So it's just the way you look at things. Stop looking at a pitch or chip as being less than one hundred percent of a swing. It is not, it is 100 percent of that particular type technique swing. So what has this to do with rhythm you might ask? It has everything to do with it. Every golfer wants to hit a golf ball as far as they can. That can only be done by using the most efficient way possible which is 80% of their rhythm, in time.

The average person can only control about 80% of their speed, (their biomechanical moves) consistently. And that 80% can only be done in their subconscious mine. If they try to control the speed in their conscious mine they may think their swing is faster but in reality the speed will be slower and out of time. This swing seems faster because it's being made with the small muscles and the small muscles sends a false signal to the conscious mind. Remember there's a lot of opposites in the game of golf and a lot of these opposites are perceived by the conscious mind. If we make our body move faster than that 80%, we will not be able to consistently control that movement. This is where the, "I don't know what happened" shots come into play. I do not teach the, "I don't know what happened", shots.

I would like you to take your time and try to understand the formula that follows. If the forward swing consists of 80% of your tempo, then that means the backswing must consist of 20%, RIGHT? Think of it this way if 20% of your tempo is used to complete the rear swing, you must have 80% left for the forward swing, Right? Because 20% + 80% equals 100% and you cannot have more than 100% of anything!

Asa golfer, to be consistent, we must put the emphasis on the part of the swing we can control in our conscious mind. There are certain parts of the golf swing that has to become automatic or second nature; these parts are the forward swing to the #6 timing position. The backswing can be controlled. As stated above the "COMPLETE" backswing should only make up 20% of your tempo. With only 20 percent of the tempo being your "COMPLETE" backswing, the golfer can control this with the conscious mind. The forward swing consisting of 80% of your tempo, it must be controlled with your subconscious mind. ***Don't make it happen, let it happen"***. What if you take your club back 30% on your backswing? You have used 30% of your tempo! What does that leave you for your forward swing? That's right 70%. This being so, your body will have the tendency to try to over swing and make up for the lost tempo. The body will fledge, flex, snatch, jerk or do something to try and make up the lost tempo (but it cannot), when this happens you will try to surpass the 100% in the swing and lose control of the complete swing. On the other hand, if you take your backswing back 10% of your tempo, then the forward swing will be at 90% - to which the average golfer cannot control. As stated, this will make the swing very inconsistent. So put the emphasis on the backswing, making sure it is proper and allow the forward swing to happen automatically.

Now here is the question – how do I know if I am taking it back 20%? All I can tell you is – it is in your mind and when you only use the 20% in the backswing. All you do on the forward swing is, "get out of your way and let it happen". You will know it as soon as it happens!

Now you can see why tempo and rhythm in a golf swing are entirely different from each other. Tempo is God-given and should never be changed by you or anyone else! Rhythm, on the other hand, can be and must be controlled. The next time you go out to practice or play, (to get your rhythm) think to yourself 20% on the backswing just get out of the way and let the 80% come through.

After you learn the above chapter, it's important to remember that your tempo and rhythm will vary with each different technique used.

A good rule of thumb is, the closer to the hole, the closer to even the rhythm will be. This is because each technique will require it to be on tempo & rhythm, but always make sure to accelerate the club through impact. Never try to have a 50% - 50% rhythm!!! The club can never accelerate forward using a 50-50 rhythm. You can only control a golf ball with acceleration of the club head.

Full swings are a 20-80% rhythm and the putting stroke is more of a 48-52% rhythm. Allow it to adjust to fit your personality and the technique you chose.

The Swing

Before I get started explaining the single plane golf swing, let me start by saying the first golf swing was no more or less than grabbing a stick in both hands then swinging it as if he was using and axe or a long-handled hammer. The swing that the first Scottish sailor invented, hitting rocks with a funny looking stick or what Mr. Norman reinvented, after hitting millions of golf balls was the same. A motion used by the body to take a club back and forward with power in the simplest form.

If this swing is so simple then why does it take a complete book to explain it you may ask? The answer is, through years of evolution of the golf swing and its setup, it will take considerable practice not to learn the new swing, but to forget the old one. If in your past you have chopped wood with an axe or worked using a sledgehammer or maybe even played baseball, hockey or cricket you already know the swing, you just don't know you know it!

Golf is the only game I know of where you put a stick in the fingers of the hand and try to impact an object with power. Think about it, what other job you work at or any sport you play are you are trying to produce power that you hold in the fingers except golf clubs? All others are held in the palms of your hands. It is also the only game I know of where the ball is stationary and the power is produced by moving the body.

The real invention by Mr. Norman, as far as I'm concerned, was moving the club out of the lead palm of the hand and into the fingers. All the while leaving the club in the palm of the trail hand. This I believe is the real genius of the man. As will be explained in the following chapter, the lead hand controls the direction of the ball flight while the trail hand generates the power, just as in using a hammer or an axe.

Pre- Golf Warm-up, Stretching Exercises Only!!!

"Always make moves SLOW and only until tight" Do not go past TIGHT!

#1, Hold head of Driver in both hands with the handle on the ground and arm's length away from you. Angle the club towards you. Bend from the waist keeping the elbows, knees and back straight until the head is between the elbows, or as far as one can go until tight. Hold tight for 5 seconds – repeat 3 times.

#2, Hold the Driver (horizontally) behind the back with both hands on the shaft and the palms facing forward. Bend from the waist moving the shaft down the back of the legs until tight. Keep the elbows and knees straight. Hold tight for 5 seconds – repeat 3 times.

#3, Hold the Driver (horizontally) in front of the body with both hands on the shaft and shoulder width. With the palms facing down and keeping the elbows straight. Rotate from the shoulders in each direction using the rotator cups in a circle until there is a worm filling in them, (about 8-10 Revolutions).

#4, Hold the Driver with both hands over the head. Stretch the Driver as high as it will go with the feet staying on the ground. Hold tight for 5 seconds – repeat 2 times. On the 3rd time hold tight and bend to the each side, from the waist 3 times, return to start. Complete!

Again, "Always move SLOW and only bend until tight" Do not go past TIGHT!

As stated before, learning a single plane swing will not be difficult, but forgetting the one you have played for years and years would be. In order to complete your transition from conventional to single plane, it will take a lot of dedication, patience and practice. I advise all my students that, if they are committed to the single plane swing, from this day forward never swing the conventional swing again. You must commit to one or the other! I would like to take this time to say again, the conventional swing is not a bad swing, only a highly complex rotary motion swing that demands more practice than play to be able to accomplish and keep it right. The single plane swing demands more practice to learn it, but less practice to play it. Explanation, it will take more practice on your part to learn this swing because of old habits, but once the swing has been learned, one trip to the range once a month is all it usually takes to keep it right.

The Eight Positions of the Single Plane Swing and the Six Timing Positions

To learn how to swing in a single plane, you must start by understanding the eight positions of the swing and how to perform them. One of the positions I hope you have already learned – the setup, now we are down to seven so let's get started.

As stated, to make a single plane swing, all that is needed is to have the correct angles of the body and club, which will create the leverage needed to produce power. All of these positions will not make a good swing unless you have the correct timing for your swing. In this chapter, we will talk about the complete swing, putting the emphasis on timing. In the single plane swing there are seven more positions you need to learn – six of them are timing positions the other one is for power – they are as follows.

When in the correct setup, the arms, hands and the shaft of that club will create the letter "y" as seen in the picture above. We will call this - the "y" angle, more on this "y" angle later in this chapter.

Setup Position   #1 Timing Position

The first position in the swing, believe it or not, is the setup. At this point you should have already learned it; if not, go back to chapter 6. Always go from the position you have learned to the next position and hold that new position in the static for a count of five. Repeat all these exercises as much as needed in order to fully learn and understand the relationships from the previous positions to the ones you are trying to learn. Don't speed this process up, it's better to do less correctly than more incorrectly! It may be a good time to go back and review balance and posture in chapter 6.

The first movement in the golf swing is a rotation of the shoulders which will enable you to reach the #1 timing position. This movement with the shoulders will allow you to maintain the "y" angle until the hands reach the trail thigh. This is also known as a one-piece takeaway. This move is achieved by rotating the shoulders only. If needed - go back and read the Sequence of the Swing in this chapter. Note: if you make this first movement with the hands or arms instead of the shoulders your swing will be out of time and if this happens it will be almost impossible to regain the timing of the swing.

#1 Position   #2 Position

The second position is when the arms reach <u>parallel to him as if ground</u> on the back swing and the lead wrist is at a full cock. When this position the shaft will be a 90-degree angle from the lead arm and on plane. This can be done by letting the trail elbow move in, what is called a straight-line motion to the trail side while extending the lead arm fully until it is pointing away from the target. Don't make the shoulders turn to get into this position – let them turn by extending the trail arm and allow the trail elbow to relax and fold to the side, (a straight-line motion). Feel as if the lead arm is pulling the shoulder, not that the shoulders is pushing the arm. It should be noted that throughout the golf swing, the trail elbow should be lower to the ground than the lead elbow. Try to have the lead arm as straight as you can. This will be explained in the next paragraph. See the swing motion drill in chapter 18.

A problem that many golfers have is how to keep the lead arm straight. This is not too hard to do if you understand why the arm bends in the first place. For most golfers, the lead arm is a subservient arm. This means that your trail arm is your dominant arm and it will try its best to lead in the swing. If it leads in the swing, it will move the trail hand to close to your shoulder at the top of your backswing. The subservient arm will follow and the only way for it to follow is for the lead elbow to bend. So knowing this takes place, how do we keep it straight? We start by keeping the trail hand away from the trail shoulder.

Perform this drill and learn where the arms go in the backswing. Get into your setup, maintain the "y" angle of the arms and now from the wrists <u>only</u> bend them to the full wrist cocked position. When done correctly the club shaft will be at a 45° angle from your arms and pointed away from your feet but still in line as the lead forearm. Keeping the wrists cocked, rotate the shoulders to the trailside – allowing the trail elbow to bend using a straight-line motion until the lead arm is parallel to the ground and the club handle is pointing at the target line. Let me try to explain this a different way, your trail hand will move in an oblong circle as the tip of the trail elbow will move in a straight line to the side. This can be done easily as long as the trail arm is relaxed and move in conjunction to the lead arm. When in this position the club shaft will be pointing at the target line and you will be in a single plane. Feel as if the lead arm is pulling the shoulder and rear elbow into their positions. Hold this position for 10 seconds and check to make sure it is correct. See number two timing position picture below.

#2 Timing Position   Top of Back-Swing

Once the golfer has reached the #2 timing position, it is time to complete the backswing. To complete the backswing the best definition I know of is "motion to resistance". What this means is the golfer must continue making their backswing as far as they can go without moving their spinal alignment, bending the lead arm or letting the lead heel come off the ground. This is known as motion. When this is complete, you will find a tight sensation in the lead side from shoulder to hip. This is known as resistance. See motion to resistance drill in chapter 18.

Top of Back-Swing   #3 Timing Position

The 3rd timing position is keeping your wrist in the cocked position - let the shoulders rotate forward until the sternum faces the ball. This is one of the most important moves you will make in any swing!!!The arms and wrists will be in the same position at this point as they were in at the top of the back swing, only the shoulders have rotated. Note: if you stay relaxed when rotating the shoulders forward - the lower body will start a small sideways movement to support the weight transfer going to the lead side. Try to keep the hips from rotating past being square to the target line.

Note: the rotation of the shoulders may be small as in Mr. Norman's swing or large as in my swing. Please remember that Mr. Norman was 5 ft. 7 and being left handed but swinging right handed - he needed little rotation to complete his motion to resistance and as for me I am 6' 1" and am very supple which means I have a lot more rotation to complete in my motion to resistance. In other words, Mr. Norman completed his resistance with a small amount of rotation past the #2 timing position and as for me I have to have a lot more rotation to receive the same resistance.

Note: the further one goes from the second timing position to get to the full back swing will depend on the individual. Also note that the further you rotate the shoulders to complete the resistance in the backswing, the further one will have to rotate the shoulders and arms (as a single unit) forward to get back to the #3 timing position.

Only after the upper body (shoulders and arms) has completed the number three timing position will the arms start to move independently in the forward swing. Until then, they moved because of the shoulder rotation, not as an independent arm movement. This is the main reason most golfers do not have power in their swing. This movement is what is called casting. See TIMING Chapter 3 Impact Zone.

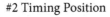

| #2 Timing Position | #3 Timing Position |

Note: there should be more of an angle from forearms to shaft upon reaching the #3 position than there was is in the #2 position. If this angle has not been achieved, there is too much wrist tension. This angle is called lagging. Lagging is important for two reasons; it shows the upper body is relaxed and ready to react to the forward motion of the swing and it helps build club head speed.

#3 Timing Position   #4 Timing Position

After learning the #3 position - allow your trail arm to start to extend as you approach the impact zone while maintaining wrist cock until which time the golf club dictates release. Try not to hold the cock in the wrist throughout this movement but learn to just relax it and let the club lead the way. It's time to explain why the impact/power zone is so difficult for most people. These difficulties are because most golfers are not taught the complete art of the golf swing which is not only the movements, but how, when and what to relax and in what order. You will find not only is it more difficult to relax than flex, but it will take longer to learn. Ever wonder why a pro or top amateur all look so smooth and fluid? It is because they have learned when and what to relax and when and what to flex. This is called timing. This is where you will gain power in the swing. Please go back and review the mental game chapter 1.

The fourth timing position is when the arms and the club shaft form the letter "y" for the third time. This will occur as the club moves though the impact zone to the lead thigh. The #4 timing position will be in line with the spinal alignment and that in also known as the bottom of the swing. To put it in a more simple way, when the arms are extended fully and form the letter "y" in front of the lead thigh, they will be directly in line with your spinal alignment. See The Nomenclature of the Impact and Power Zone Chapter 3.

#4 Timing Position   #5 Timing Position

The fifth timing position is when both arms are parallel to the ground and the shaft of the club is pointed at the target. To reach this position, all that needs to be done is to let your lead elbow relax and bend close to the side. Note: at this time, both feet are still flat on the ground if possible. It is also important to remember that although the feet are flat on the ground they do not have roots. What this means is that although your feet are on the ground for balance - they must be able to operate and move when necessary.

#5 Timing Position   #6 Timing Position

The 6th timing position is not really a timing position per-say, but only the complete follow through to a relaxed finish. This has been achieved when the weight of the body is on the outside of the lead foot and the toe of the trail foot is on the ground while the sole of the foot is facing away from the target. I believe this is one of the most complex but easiest positions to learn. What this means is that you must do two things at the same time all while performing one of the easiest moves in the game of golf. These two things are allowing the trail elbow to relax and bend and the trail heel to come off the ground at the same time, then letting them to go to their completion. I say again, <u>never stop a swing - let it stop itself!</u> What makes it easy you might wonder? It is simply because this move is so easy on the body that the body will crave it if only you can relax enough and practice correctly.

How can you produce power in your golf swing?

One of the most frequently asked questions we get as instructor's is "HOW CAN I GET MORE DISTANCE," or, better yet – "WHY CAN'T I GET MORE DISTANCE?" Most golfers think they have to swing their hands and arms faster to have more power. But not necessarily – if your hands and arms get too fast, you will not be able to control them!

In this chapter, I will explain why the core of the swing (the spinal column) is so important and how the speed of the swing is determined by the core's rotation. To put it another way – the farther away your shoulders, arms, and hands are from the core of the swing, the faster they have to move to stay in time with (some may say stay connected with) the core.

Although some will say that they would rather have consistency over distance, they still try to hit the ball farther. I too think that consistency is better than distance (particularly if you cannot control your distance), but in golf – distance with control is the Holy Grail. One must remember that distance is relative to the individual golfer. **NOTE:** What is the right distance for one golfer will not be the right distance for all. Even professional golfers on tour don't hit the ball the same distance. I must say that if you are happy with your distance and you can control it – don't change what you are doing. It's too hard to get back to where you were if you keep trying something new that doesn't work.

Too many golfers try to swing with memory – not with reality. What is meant by that is, at some point in their past, they played golf in what is called "the zone" – a state of mind where the subconscious mind make the swing. They had a great round of golf or they made a very long drive and they think – this is my game! Well, I hate to break it to them, but that is not their game – although it could be if they will take the time to go back and really learn to do consistently what they were doing when they were in "the zone." Most will not.

One of the biggest flaws is to focus on results instead of concentrating on execution. If a golfer focus on results without concentrating on execution, the results may or may not be accomplished – if they are, that's called a miracle shot. I don't teach miracle shots, I teach consistency! I'm not interested in teaching someone to, as they say, "put the cart before the horse." Until the golfer has practiced enough to make the execution automatic, the results should always come <u>after</u> correct execution. But what if there was a way to be both consistent and get more distance? Simply put – there is. The first thing we need to do, however, is to learn what I call the Nomenclature of the Golf Swing is described in chapter 3 impact zone. Next we need to marry the impact zone and the power zone. Study the picture below, and then let's gets started!

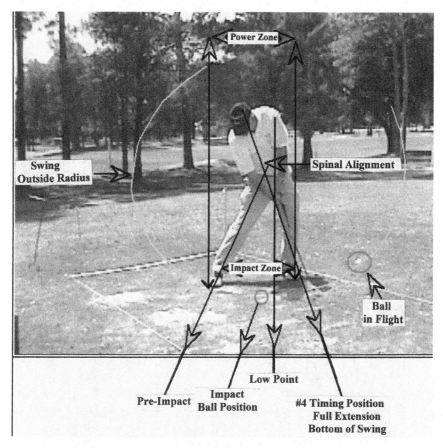

The Nomenclature of the Golf Swing

As stated, power in the golf swing is the product of using three things: angles, leverage, and timing in the impact zone – all three related to a fixed core. To learn how to swing a golf club with power, one must first know what to do in that swing to achieve that power. Look at the picture above and see just what needs to happen to generate power. As you can see, to achieve power in the swing one must learn how to marry the impact zone and the power zone. First, to understand what happens in the impact zone one must learn about three things: angles, leverage, and timing. Before I explain them, we must say more about the most misunderstood fundamental, which is – what drives the swing is the core!

The Core (Spinal Column)

To learn how to make a more powerful golf swing, one must first learn how to rotate instead of directionally moving the core and fully understand why rotating instead of moving directionally is so important! The core of any golf swing is the spinal column. This is why <u>getting and maintaining spinal alignment throughout the swing</u> is so important.

Setup   Impact

As you can see in the above pictures, the spine is aligned when there is a straight line from your tailbone right through your head, I say again – through the head– through the head– through the head. Pardon the repetition, but it's so important that the straight line extends through the head. So keep your head aligned with your spine! I will write more about this later in this chapter, but first things first.

The spinal column is not part of the lower body, so why do we think we need to start the swing with the lower body first? We don't! As stated in the chapter on sequence of the single plane golf swing – the mind leads and the body follows.

We start the swing by using our minds. Ask yourself is the setup complete and correct? Only after the answer is "yes" should the swing be initiated! At this point the body starts it rotation around the core, (The spinal column). The spinal column should not move directionally – rather it rotates around an axis. The farther the parts of the swing are from the core, the more speed and the more power can be produced. As seen in the picture below.

#3Timing position   Impact

Mr. Moe Norman

If you will look closely at the above pictures, you can see in the forward swing that from the #3 timing position to the <u>impact position</u> (not to be confused with full extension) Mr. Norman's spinal alignment has not changed – his spine has only rotated. In the picture you can also see that his sternum has moved forward about four inches while his trail elbow has moved forward about one foot and his hands about three feet, but look at the club head – it has moved about twelve feet. It is important to note that at impact, his hands are still in front of the club head and the trail wrist is not extended fully. This is because his arms and wrists do not start their uncoiling until the last possible moment going into the impact zone. When you are able to achieve this timing as he has – you will have married the two zones. Full extension will only happen at the # 4 timing position (see picture – Nomenclature of the Golf Swing).

So, as stated before, the core (spinal column) only rotates, and the speed of the swing is determined by the speed of that rotation. To speed up the swing, don't try to speed up the hands or arms – simply rotate the core faster and allow the body to move with it. In other words – don't make the arms and hands move more quickly in the forward swing, allow them to follow the core.

In my teaching, this is the one fundamental that I find is most misunderstood! I know I keep writing about this and it may sound a little like overkill, but it is too important not to stress! So here it is again, if the core moves directionally instead of rotating – it will be almost impossible to get back to the proper impact position consistently, because it is the rotation of the spinal column that stabilizes the golf swing. If the core moves directionally instead of rotating in the swing, then the center of the swing will move and all the fundamentals you spent so much time learning will be for nothing. Another way to think about this is – just as in a circle there is a center that all rotates around (think of a bicycle wheel revolving around its hub), in the swing this center is the spinal column (the core). The more the center of the wheel moves - the bumpier the ride.

The last thing needs to be said about the core is this – the core also needs to rotate in a steady motion throughout the swing – not in a stop and go or jerky motion but with a smooth continuous flowing motion. (See Tempo &Rhythm – Chapter 8). Think about the bicycle wheel – **the smoother the rotation - the smoother the ride**.

Now it is time to start talking about angles, leverage, and timing. We will start with angles, then move to leverage and on to timing.

ANGLES

The "y" Angle

The angle we will talk about is called the "*y*" angle. Let's take a moment and explain what is meant by the term "*y*" angle. To get the proper setup, one must start with the lead side. With the <u>lead</u> arm, we want the line of the shaft and the extended lead arm to form a straight line from the shoulder to the blade of the club. The trail <u>hand</u> is placed on the grip under the lead hand approximately 3" to 4" lower on the shaft than your lead hand.

With the trail hand this much lower than the lead hand and a straight line from the shoulder to the blade of the club, when looking from a position in line with the target, but from the trail side of the golfer – this will be the foundation for the "y angle." The angles formed by the lead arm and shaft along with the trail arm will form the letter "*y*" at the setup position. (See pictures below.)

Setup

As stated the 1st "*y*" is at address (setup), as stated above. Notice how much lower the trail shoulder is than the lead shoulder, the tilt of the upper body, and the spinal alignment. Also note where the head is; somewhere over the trail knee.

The 2ⁿᵈ "*y*" (#1 timing position) is when the arms reach the trail thigh on the backswing. This is called "the one-piece takeaway." This movement is so important that I will explain it again. The one-piece takeaway is <u>not</u> a movement of the arms or wrist but of the <u>shoulders</u>. Although this movement is small, it is one of the most important movements in the golf swing when it comes to the timing of the swing; <u>it must not be overlooked.</u> This movement sets up the timing of the complete golf swing – without it the swing will start out of time. If timing is not maintained, the golfer will have the tendency to release the trail wrist early on the forward swing, causing what is called "casting the club." This early release is most often caused by being out of time and <u>subconsciously</u> trying to regain the timing by using the forearms instead of the shoulders, to start the forward swing. When this happens the golfer will no longer be accelerating the club through the impact zone but will be shoving the club with hands and arms, which will reduce the power of the swing. When this happens, the club cannot be accelerated <u>through</u> the impact zone but rather accelerated "<u>to</u>" the impact zone.

The 3rd "*y*" is when the arms on the forward part of the swing are extended fully in front of the lead thigh and is in line with your core (spine), which has spinal alignment. This is also known as the #4 timing position. When this is achieved, the club will be accelerating <u>through</u> impact, not <u>to</u> impact! If there is a loss of distance, a good thing to look for is the "*y*" angle having been reached too early in the forward swing.

It has been said that the single plane swing is an arm-generated body motion. But, as explained above, the shoulders initiate the arms. When making this movement, the body will move in "anticipation of," and in "support of," the upper body movement. It might be said that the single plane swing is a shoulder-initiated, arm-generated body movement. Without this shoulder movement, the timing in the golf swing (without an early release) will be almost impossible to accomplish. This is why the "*y*" angle is so important in all three positions of the swing, and also to develop the leverage that is needed to get the power and distance we are looking for. When doing these movements one must not forget to stay in the correct balance and posture as stated in chapter 6 setup.

Leverage

We achieve leverage in the golf swing by using a double lever system. Let me explain what is meant by the term double lever system when it comes to the human body. First, what the difference between a single lever and double lever? A single lever can best be described as a single straight rod from tip to tip. It can only move in a single line from its pivot point. Here's an example – if you hold one tip of the rod and swing it, you will see that it can only move to form an angle with the point you are holding – a pendulum is a great example. When swinging a single lever, it is easy to maintain a single plane – but you cannot produce enough club head speed and force to create enough power. When swinging a double lever it is easier to generate club head speed and force to get power, but it's not as easy to maintain a single plane. The reason for this is the movement of the arms during the double lever swing. With this in mind, let me explain the double lever and how to use it to maintain a single plane swing. (See picture below)

The Double Lever in the Swing

A double lever has two straight rods joined together in the middle by a swivel joint. When using the body to form a double lever, the lead arm and the shaft comprise the two rods. Just as a mechanical double lever has a swivel point between the two rods, the wrist is the swivel point for the body. The wrist should remain flexible but not totally limp, just relaxed. A problem that some golfers have is how to keep the lead arm straight. This is not too hard to do if you understand why the arm bends in the first place. For most golfers, the lead arm is a subservient arm. This means that your trail arm is your dominant arm and it will try to lead in the swing. If it leads in the swing, it will move the hand too close to your shoulder at the top of your backswing. The subservient arm will follow and the only way for it to follow is for the lead elbow to bend. So knowing this takes place, how do we keep it straight? We start by keeping the trail hand away from the trail shoulder.

Perform this drill and you can learn where the arms go in the backswing, how to maintain a straight lead arm, and where the trail elbow is positioned.

Get into your setup. Maintaining the first "y" angle and the correct balance and posture, from the wrists <u>only</u> bend them to the fully cocked position. At this point the club shaft will be pointed away from you at a 45-degree angle, but still in line as the lead forearm. You may have noticed that this is the same drill as the wrists cock drill as stated in chapter 6 set up. Keeping the wrists cocked, rotate the shoulders to the trailside – allowing the trail elbow to bend in a straight angle to the side until the lead arm is parallel to the ground and the club handle is pointing at the target line. In this position, with the club shaft pointing at the target line, you will be able to maintain a single plane.

The outside tip of a double lever will move its fastest in the forward swing during spinal rotation – both rods become a straight line as the swivel joint (wrists) uncocks. Correct timing of a golf swing will mean that this straight line is achieved when the club impacts the ball. The laws of physics (if allowed to) will straighten out a double lever automatically at the heaviest point of the swing. When the swing is in time, the heaviest and lowest point of the swing will marry and become one because of gravity. If the golfer relaxes his wrists and allows the two levers to work properly, then they will have the tendency to straighten themselves out at the lowest point, which happens to be under the lead shoulder's rotator cuff. Knowing this leads to some very interesting questions. One of these questions is: if the double lever is extended to its fullest at the low point, how can the club head be accelerating through impact and still reach its maximum speed past impact (that is, at extension)? I answer this way – because although a double lever will have the tendency to straighten it out at the low point, normal ball position is 2 inches behind the low position of the swing and the trail arm is not fully extended at this position and will not be until it reaches the bottom of the swing, number four timing position. Again, see the picture on the nomenclature of the golf swing for the low and bottom point of the swing.

I know I keep saying the same things over and over, but that's how important I think they are.

In the conventional swing, there are two elements in the swing that will create energy transfer from the head of the club to the golf ball. These two elements are – the mass of the club head and the speed at which the club head is moving! In a single plane swing, these two elements are assisted by a third. This third element is the extension of the trail arm through impact – which is what produces force. In the single plane swing, this force is what is known as the Hammer Effect. This Hammer Effect is the true secret to the power of a single plane swing. The trail arm is not a lever but because of the trail hand Palm grip it becomes a power source. The trail arm has nothing to do in the back swing except fold naturally. In the forward swing all the movement of the trail arm is between the numbers three and number four timing positions allowing the single plane to extend into to create the force needed to produce the power. In the single plane swing this is what's known as the hammer affect.

As stated before in this book, and I know it's hard to believe, I have found more power when using the single plane swing versus the conventional swing. Using the same club and the same club head speed, the ball will travel approximately one club longer using a single plane swing versus the conventional swing for most golfers when performed correctly. I contribute this to the extension of the trail arm <u>through</u> impact – not <u>to</u> impact – which leads us to "timing"!

The Six Timing Positions of the Single Plane Swing

The golfer can build club head speed with timing. Timing can best be described as having the correct angles at the correct positions of the swing in order to create leverage.

As stated, to make a ball go a long way, all that is needed is to have the correct angles, leverage, and timing. As you can see from the picture above all timing is having the correct angles at the correct positions throughout the complete swing. If this is not understood I suggest you go back to the sequence of the swing earlier in this chapter when all timing positions have been explained thoroughly.

Now that you have learned all about angles, leverage and timing and you have also learned how to marry the impact zone and the power zone, go out there and boom it!

Chapter 8

ALIGNMENT TO
THE TARGET

After learning the correct setup and swing, the biggest problems most golfers have in advancing the ball toward the target can be traced to the alignment of the body relative to that target. The theory behind body alignment to the target can best be described as the railroad effect. Many instructors have emphasized this over the years. Although this is the correct method in setting up your alignment to the target, it will not help you unless you have the understanding of that method and a simple way of obtaining it so that your practice session will be from the correct position without having to stand on a railroad track. In this chapter, I will explain why we need to be in this position and a simple and easy way to practice and achieve it when playing. I do not think the human body and mind will allow one to achieve the perfect position every time, the touring professionals come as close as any to achieving it but even they cannot accomplish it every time.

When getting the alignment to the target, most golfers tend to make the same mistake. This mistake is looking at the target as they address the ball. When this happens, the body will line itself to the target; this has to do with the eyes. As stated in chapter9, your eyes are the most dominant sense you have in your body. This is why if you look at that the target when getting your address – your body will align itself to the target putting your swing out of alignment.

This alignment of the body to the target will influence an over the top move or what is called outside to inside swing path, (See Ball Flight Laws). This is done because the golfer has a habit of aligning the body first and then adjusting the face of the golf club and the swing path to fit that incorrect body alignment. Just the opposite should happen when getting into the proper alignment.

I instruct my students just to think about <u>what</u> they're trying to hit the ball with. What hits the ball is the face of the club; not your body. This being so, what should be aimed at the target? The answer is simple, <u>the face of the golf club,</u> (see the chapter on the impact zone). So if the face of the club is what hits the ball - shouldn't we make sure the clubface is aimed at the target? This being so doesn't <u>it</u> stand to reason that we should work <u>from the clubface to the body</u> when getting the correct alignment?

First I will explain the proper alignment of both the face of the club and the body. Second I will outline a good setup routine in order to practice and learn the proper alignment.

An easy way to understand what happens when you get alignment looking at the target is to stand and face the target. Using the arms as gauges, the left arm will be your body alignment to the target while the right arm will signify the path of the club to the target, (lefts will have to reverse). While standing and facing the target, raise the <u>left</u> arm and point the index finger at the target; this will be body alignment to the target. This alignment of the body to the target is what happens when you look at the target while addressing the ball. Next, raise the right arm and point the right index finger at the same target. This right arm will signify the path of the club as it goes toward the target. With both arms in place you will notice that the arms are not on parallel lines with each other– as needed in the golf swing - but rather on converging lines. These converging lines will show that the path of the club, (the right arm) to be from outside to inside path when compared with the left arm alignment, (the body). Revisit the <u>Ball flight laws in chapter 1</u> to fully understand what will happen with an outside to inside path of the club. Again, this is the major mistake most weekend golfers make when getting their line to the target and why most golfers slices the ball.

To get the proper alignment, do the following, again stand and face the target and but this time raise and point the <u>right</u> index finger at the target; this again will signify the path of the club. Next raise the left arm and point the index finger down range leaving both arms on parallel lines to each other. This will be your body alignment. When this is done, you will notice that the left arm, (body alignment) will <u>not</u> be in line with the target, but actually pointed to the left of the target down range. This is what is meant by the railroad effect.

How can we practice in our set up to get the correct alignment? By using some irons in your bag we can make an alignment gauge that can be used on the driving range to practice the correct setup alignment to the target; this is how it is done. Note: do this enough when you practice until you don't need them and can get into the correct alignment automatically.

Body alignment Target line

First, using a club, lay it on the ground with the grip pointed towards the target. Next, lay another club on the ground to the left with the grip pointed down range and parallel line to the first club. The right side club on the ground will signify the path of the club and the second club, the one on the left, will signify the body alignment. You will notice that the left club, (body alignment club) is pointed down range and pointed left of the target.

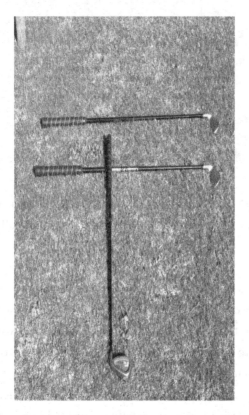

Next, place a third club on a right angle to the 2nd club with the grip pointing away from the body. This club will signify the center of the body and proper ball position.

Remove the first club. Assume your setup position with your feet evenly spaced away from the body alignment club. Place the ball in front of the grip and make a swing down range hitting the ball to the target.

When making any adjustments to the setup or swing, there will be a certain amount of transitional time to be expected. It seems to me that the older we get, the longer the transition time between where we <u>are</u> and where we <u>need</u> to be. Knowing this, just stay patient and committed to the change; it will happen. You will notice that when hitting balls for the first several times in this position, the balls will tend to go left of target (for right-handers). This is to be expected because old habits die hard. It will take time to correct the flaws in the swing so just be aware of this and have patience. To hasten this time, a good drill to do is - once you get in your setup and your alignment, simply looks at the target direction then back to the ball, back to the target direction, back to the ball and then swing. Don't take more than 20 sec. from the time you last look at the direction you wish to swing to and the swing itself. If one gets in the habit of doing this, it makes the transition from where you were, to where you want to be, a lot quicker. When performing this drill always have a target. <u>This is done because we need to be thinking of the ball flight to the target - not of the swing!</u> Repeat this drill until you can take it to the golf course and knock down some pins.

Chapter 9

YOU'RE OPTICS

Since the start of the game of golf, someone has said, "keep your eye on the ball". You also have heard, "look at the back of the ball". These tips may be OK for the traditional golf swing but is bad information when it comes to the single plane swing. The traditional golf swing is a descending striking swing from inside the target line. ***The single plane swing is a sweeping descending swing from down the line.*** The line we are referring to is not the target line but the swing plane line. The best definition of a swing plane is a circular motion always in line with itself. The best example of this is the pendulum. In a true pendulum motion, the shaft of the pendulum is always in line with itself. When the shaft of the true pendulum motion is 180 degrees out from its bottom, it is still in line with itself. Each club in our bag has a different lie angle, loft angle, length and flex of the shaft. With a different lie angle, the club must be tilted on an axis to accommodate that lie angle. This is what is referred to as shaft plane. In the single plane swing the shaft plane and the swing plane are one in the same, so in a true single plane swing, when the shaft plane moves to accommodate the club head the shaft angle, the arm plane must move with it to form the single plane. What does this have to do with your optics? Well, you must first know the main difference between the traditional swing and the single plane swing.

Your eyes are the most dominant sense you have in your body. 80 to 85% of all the knowledge you have acquired in your life has come from your eyes.

This is why your optics are so important in your golf swing. Your hand-eye coordination has always worked on a horizontal plane. This is one reason your final look at your target should be on a horizontal plane.

In the traditional swing, we are taught that the outside of our feet at address is roughly that of our shoulders with our lead foot flared approximately 20 to 25 degrees toward the target. The sole of the club should be flat to ground and square to the line at address. The arms are hanging straight under the shoulders and the grip of the club is in the fingers of your hands. This creates an angle between the arms and the shaft. This angle is what causes all the problems in the traditional swing. When you swing a club around your body, the club head grows in inertia weight. The faster you swing the club, the heavier the club becomes. At one hundred miles per hour, the club head grows from one and one-half pounds of dead weight to 65 lb. of the inertia weight. This 65 pounds of inertia weight will have the arms straighten themselves out at the heaviest point of the golf swing (the bottom). As the arms straighten out at the bottom of the swing, the outside radius of the golf swing in its forward motion grows approximately 3 ½" to 4 ½". With this growth of the outside radius at the bottom of the swing, the traditional golfer must initiate the downswing with the drive of the legs towards the target which in turn rotates the pelvis toward the target, or what is referred to as clearing the hips. Clearing the hips relieves pressure in the upper body so the golfer can rotate around the spinal column and raise his lead shoulder away from the target line just enough to accommodate the growth in the outside radius at the bottom of the swing. The traditional golf swing radius looks like the letter "U". This makes the traditional swing a dissenting striking swing. With this type swing, the golfer can look at the back of the ball and make solid contact because the club is on a descending path. In contrast to the traditional swing, the single plane golf swing is a sweeping, slightly descending swing.

When setting up in the single plane, at address the arms plane and club shaft plane are in line with themselves. When the shaft plane is the same as your swing plane, the outside radius at the bottom of the swing cannot grow. If the radius cannot grow, then the golfer does not need to raise his lead shoulder away from the target line at the moment of impact. If the golfer does not need to raise the shoulder then he does not need to rotate their hips and there is no need to drive with their legs. So one can see all of these movements are not necessary to consistently hit a golf ball when using a single plane swing. This is the biggest difference between the two swings and why the single plane swing is easier to learn and keep. The arc of the natural swing looks like an inverted "C" or like you are standing in a bowl swinging around the bottom of that bowl. This means the angle of approach of the club head is more sweeping than the traditional descending swing. Which leads us back to the optics of the golfer. If the golfer looks at the top of the ball and tries to hit the bottom of the ball, there will be a one and three-quarters inch depth perception flaw in their set up. If the golfer looks at the back of the ball, there will be a one inch depth perception flaw in their set up. The essence of hitting a golf ball is to have the blade flat to the ground square to the line moving down that line with enough accelerating club head speed to project the ball to its target. If the club is flat to the ground and the ball is flat on the ground, then the club will contact the ball at about the 3rd or 4th line up from the bottom on the face of a club. If the golfer looks at the top of the ball and swings to the bottom of the ball, they will have a tendency to blade or top the ball. Try to play darts looking at a spot 2" left of center and hit center or play horseshoes looking at a spot 2 ft. right of the stake and hit the stake; "almost impossible". ***But in the single plane golf swing, we keep looking at something we are not swinging at, all the time wondering why we can't hit what we want???*** To produce a solid impact of the ball, the golfer must return the club under the ball at moment of impact. So doesn't it make sense to look at what you are swinging at? With the human's hand-eye coordination as it is, this is almost impossible to do while looking at the top or the back of the golf ball trying to hit the bottom. We must try to **look under the ball**, not at it. Here is a good drill to accomplish solid contact. First place a tee in the ground at grass level. Make a full swing and try to clip the tee out of the ground. Focus only on the tee and only hit the tee out of the ground. Swing until you only hit the tee. Next place another tee in the ground about one-half inch to trail side of the first tee and place a ball on the forward tee. Swing and look at the trail tee, not at the ball. This would get your focus under the ball not at it. The golfer should never try to hit a ball but only to make a good swing. Too many times we try to hit a golf ball instead of making a good swing. Try not to be hit-oriented or ball-fixated but instead try to be swing-oriented. Get into the correct setup then make a good swing and the hit will happen. Because the golfers you play with will not let you put a tee in the ground while you are playing (they are funny that way), try to pick out a spot under the ball (behind the ball) on the ground as close to the ball as you can see and that becomes your tee. A light spot, dark spot, blade of grass, grain of sand, anything; this becomes your focal point, not the ball. Mr. Norman said, he never looks at the ball, he always looks under the ball!

Your eye position is very important when getting the correct setup. When you obtain the correct set up position, your eyes will be approximately 4" behind your ball position. This will put your head somewhere over your trail knee. In this position, your lead shoulder is about 1" to 2" forward of your ball at address. This puts the bottom of the swing about 1" to 2" forward of the ball. Remember us as single plane golfers will swing around our lead shoulder and not around our eyes. Remember the low point in the swing is directly under the lead shoulder (see nomenclature of the golf swing, Chapter 3 Impact Zone). Your shoulders and your spinal column are connected by bone and will only move up and down and back and forth in relationship to each other, they cannot move into or away from your spine. With this being so, if you allow your head to move forward on your forward swing, then your lead shoulder must move with it. This will have you swinging on a descending plane with a de-lofted club face because the bottom of the swing will move forward with your head. Your optics have not always been the center of your world; your hand-eye coordination put your eyes in the center of your world. Your eyes are not the center of your single plane swing, they are only a focal point that keeps the center of your swing, your lead shoulder, in position. This eye position will also help you to look under the ball throughout your swing.

A good drill to achieve this is to spray paint a line about 3 feet long on the ground and another one about 4 inches to the rear of the first line. Place your ball on the 1st line and keep your eyes over the 2nd line as you hit balls off the 1st. line. This will help train you to keep your head back over your trail knee and help maintain a straight spinal column. So as you may see, your optics are very important to your golf swing. The next time you play golf, remember your optics and the role they play in your swing.

HOW TO TAKE YOUR SWING FROM THE DRIVING RANGE TO THE GOLF COURSE

As Mr. Norman has said many times, the longest walk in golf is from the practice tee to the first tee.

Too many times, we as golfers will hit the ball great on the driving range but can't do the same on the golf course. Why? Maybe it's because of the way we practice. We go to the driving range, pick our best club, hit it until it feels great and then pull out the driver and see how far we can hit it. That's not practice, it is exercise". Let's start a good practice routine so we can do two things, 1st learn how to make a good swing, 2nd learn how to take our swing to the golf course.

Start out by getting you a small notebook pad and keep it in your golf bag at all times. Take a bucket of golf balls and make two piles of balls. Just say there are 80 balls in the bucket. Divide the balls, 60 in one pile and 20 in the other. Cover the 20 with the empty bucket so you have to make a move

117

to get to the 20. Practice with the 60 balls. Make a mental box all around you. All your concentration and thoughts stay inside the box. You can make your mental box any color you want it to be, (mine is usually blue, sometimes it's red) because only you can see it. Keep all your practices in that box, (physical and mental), at this point you don't care where the ball goes or how well you strike it. The ball is only a focal point and not something you are trying to hit to any target, it doesn't matter where the ball goes! You do not have a target! Now pick a particular piece of your golf swing that you want to practice. Say your takeaway, for instance or maybe your lower body set up – any piece of your swing that you feel you don't have right or you fell is not working. Practice with all of the balls in this pile without caring about ball flight. Just practice *one* particular piece at a time until it is a habit and it repeats. AGAIN, don't worry about where the ball goes; don't think about the target. Just practice one piece at a time and stay in the box.

After you finish with the pile of 60 or it becomes a habit and will repeat, uncover the 2nd pile of 20. Now completely change your mental process. Step out of the box, the box does not exist anymore, (until you need it again). Pretend that you are out on the golf course. Forget about your swing and think, TARGET, TARGET, TARGET. Play each shot to a different target and with a different club. Never hit at the same target twice in a row, never hit the same club twice in a row and never hit the same shot twice in a row even if you whiff it. One target, one club, one swing and only one chance to hit it at your target. You don't do it on the golf course so don't do it here! Play your shots as if you were on the golf course not on the driving range.

Now is when the notebook pad comes in. Watch your shots and see what they are doing. Are they going at the target, are they going right, left or whatever? Let's say your ball is going to the left of your target. If you are going to play at this time do not to try to fix it during play, play with what you have! If you are not going to play, it is time to get back into the box and repeat the above. In either case, take out your notebook pad and write down the date, write the word practice and what your tendencies are, pulling left or pushing right, whatever it is. Put the notebook pad in your golf bag.

The next time you go to play golf, what are you going to do? Take out your notebook pad and see what your tendencies were, (going left!). Worm yourself up before you play to see if you are doing the same as your last practice and if it is, are you going to play the ball to the middle of the fairway? NO! Play your ball to the right side of the fairway. Don't fight it, play it!

When your game is over, (before you go to the 19th hole) take out your notebook pad and write down the date, write, play and what you were doing in your round (pulling left). Put it back in your golf bag.

WHAT ARE YOU GOING TO PRACTICE IN THE BOX THE NEXT TIME YOU GO THE DRIVING RANGE??? WHY AM I PULLING THE BALL LEFT?

Keep doing this and you will be able to take the driving range to the golf course but remember, practice with a purpose, practice with a goal, but most importantly, only practice one thing at a time.

PRACTICE ON THE PRACTICE RANGE,
PLAY ON THE GOLF COURSE
NOT THE OTHER WAY AROUND.

JUNIOR GOLFERS

Politicians love to talk about how the future of our country rests on the shoulders of today's children.

The same can be said about golf. The future of golf is in the hands - or swing, we might say - of our junior golfers who roam the fairways today. The more junior golfers there are today, the brighter the future will be tomorrow, and for this reason alone, it is important to have a strong junior golf program.

I believe in the youngsters of today. I also believe there are better ways than others to introduce our children or grandchildren to the game. With that in mind, let's talk about what I see as a good junior golf program and how to get a youngster involved in golf while having fun at the same time.

The most frequently asked question I get from parents and grandparents is when and where the best time and place is to get a junior involved in golf. My answer is always the same: You need to expose your juniors as soon as you can and encourage them. The place is anywhere they can safely hit a golf ball, whether it's the backyard, an open field or even a driving range. Just make sure it's "safe" - where they can't hit anyone or anything, and they won't feel intimidated by other people.

After that, simply back off and leave them alone and let them have some fun. When they come back and ask you for some instruction, then you will know they are ready for the next step and will put the effort into learning.

The key here is that learning more about the game has to be their idea - they can't be pushed into it. If the interest continues, seek out a good junior golf program and get him or her into it.

This game of golf is such an individual sport that it takes a lot of desire and discipline to learn. Juniors have to have the desire to succeed, and if they are pushed into it, they may not have the desire that it takes to learn and stick with the game. Remember, playing and learning golf must be fun for the junior player. Otherwise, they may lose interest and move on to other sports that seem more fun to them.

One of the things I love most about being a single plane golf instructor is giving a golf club to junior players who have not been instructed on how to hit a golf ball. I'll tell them to take a whack at the ball, and it's amazing what happens next: their feet spread wide, the club goes into the palms of their hands and their arms form a straight line to the ball as they take the club back and swing.

Sounds like single plane golf, doesn't it? It's funny what people will or will not do - until "someone" tells them they can't do it that way.

If you're trying to get a youngster started in golf, here are a few things that go into making a good junior golf program:

- ☐ Start out by teaching golf course etiquette.
- ☐ Pick a rule of golf to talk about before each lesson.
- ☐ Teach the fundamentals of golf (preferably single plane, but don't force it).
- ☐ Teach how to have fun while playing and practicing.
- ☐ Teach the drills in a way that is fun for the junior.

☐ Take it slow - one thing at a time.
☐ Make sure the junior has clubs that fit and are not too heavy for him or her.
☐ put the juniors in a class with youngsters of the same age group.
☐ Have a dress code.
☐ Get their commitment, no matter what their age. You can even have them sign a Junior Golf Rules "contract" and have them abide by it. Help them to remember the rules by going over them before each class, but only talk about six or seven rules and make them simple. If you do more than that, they become a chore and not a game.
☐ finally, always remember they are Junior Golfers!

If we do the above things, we have a good chance that our beloved game will be here for a long time and continue to grow and grow.

Someone once said there would never be another Hogan. Then came Palmer. There would never be another Palmer, and then came Nicklaus. There would never be another Nicklaus, and then - BOOM - came Tiger.

Some people say there will never be another Moe Norman. But I say, "Just wait..."

The Single Plane Golfing Juniors are coming!

Chapter 12

EQUIPMENT

Just as there are differences in golf swings, so are there differences in golf equipment. Let me start by saying that all equipment should be fitted to the golfer and the swing that the golfer use. A certified teaching professional or a certified club fitter should fit clubs. I am a firm believer that the easiest thing to get right in golf is the equipment; the hardest thing to get right is the golf SWING!!!

There has been a lot of confusion about golf swings and how (or if) the equipment has been designed for particular swings. In this chapter, I will explain why and how equipment was designed to assist these swings.

One of the first questions golfers ask is – can I make a single plane swing with conventional clubs? The answer is yes, just as you can eat a steak with a butter knife, or soup with a teaspoon, but it is a lot easier and more efficient to use the right equipment.

To make a single plane swing using conventional golf clubs requires knowledge of some things that can happen to the ball in flight. When making the correct single plane swing, but using a golf club designed for the conventional swing, the ball will have the tendency to go to the right of the target (for a right-handed golfer) on most off-centered hits. A lot of this can be attributed to the swing, although engineering plays a big role. Unless you can hit the ball in the sweet spot every time, you will have to make adjustments to the alignment of your body to the target to accommodate a possible off-centered hit.

I will explain some of the properties of the two swings along with the equipment best designed for them. Let's start with the swings, then move on to the club heads, the shafts, and finally the grips.

The Swings

Set-up   Impact

The Conventional Swing

Set-up   Impact

The Single Plane Swing

This is unlike the single plane swing, where most of the rotation occurs outside (behind) the impact zone. Another way to think about it this is – the club head will mirror the hands, and because the hands rotate as they move though the impact zone in the conventional swing, so will the club head. In either swing, there is about 180 degrees of rotation of the club head; it's just where the rotation takes place in each of the swings!!!

Pre-impact   Impact   Full Extension

The Conventional Swing

In the conventional golf swing, (because of the two plane setup) the rotation of the club head through the impact zone will only allow the face of the club to be square to the target line for 2–4", (for the average golfer). See picture above. The clubs best designed for that conventional swing are toe-weighted clubs; toe weighting promotes club head rotation. That rotation is necessary for the club head to achieve that 2–4" of square tracking. It's because of this limited square tracking distance that most off-centered hits will go anywhere but down the target line.

Pre-impact   Impact   Full Extension

The Single Plane Swing

In the single plane swing, because of its setup the rotation occurs outside of (behind) the impact zone. In the <u>forward</u> swing, the club head has almost completed its rotation by the time it gets to the start of the impact zone. As stated before, the club head will mirror the hands. Therefore, because the hands rotate outside the impact zone in the single plane swing, so will the club head. From the trail foot to the ball, the club head will only rotate about 10 degrees, compared to the 80 to 90 degrees of rotation in the conventional golf swing in the same area. <u>See picture above</u>. As stated before, <u>the impact zone is all that matters!</u> The club head of the single plane golf swing will stay square to the target line between 12–16" compared to 2–4" for the conventional golf swing. The fact that most of the rotation in the single plane swing occurs outside the impact zone has led to the term square tracking. A center-weighted club will promote this square tracking, just as the toe-weighted club promotes the club head rotation of the conventional swing in the impact zone. Not only does the center-weighted club head designed for the single plane swing promote square tracking, that same center weighting means that most off-centered hits will be out of trajectory, not off line.

The Club Heads

If you look closely, you can see that there is a big difference between clubs designed for the conventional swing and clubs designed for the single plane swing. For example, there are differences in the club head, the shaft, and the grip. The pictures below show the differences in club heads.

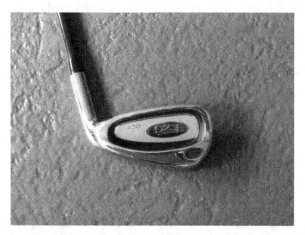

A conventional toe-weighted club head.

The Natural Golf center-weighted club head.

To put it simply, the chief differences between conventional clubs and clubs designed to facilitate a single plane swing are the weighting of the head, the shape of the grip, and the torque of the shaft. A conventional club has toe-weighted club heads, tapered grips, and shafts with higher torque. Some conventional club manufacturers are now making their clubs with lower torque shafts; this will help some with off-centered hits, but the problem remains that the conventional clubs produce only 2–4" of square tracking through the impact zone in the swing. Clubs designed for the single plane swing have center-weighted club heads, non-tapered grips, and shafts with lower torque. It is also worth noting that the hosel of the center-weighted clubs is shortened. This allows the club maker to move more weight behind the sweet spot of the club, for more swing weight in the head and to lighten the overall weight of the club. One thing that had to be done because of the short hosel is to make the end of the shaft with lower torque.

The Grips

A Single Plane non-tapered Grip

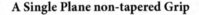

A Conventional Tapered Grip

The grip on the conventional club is tapered. This is because the grip goes in the fingers of the trail hand to allow the two-plane setup. There has been a lot of confusion about why the grip on the old Natural Golf clubs, which are designed to facilitate the single plane swing, are non-tapered. In fact, the grip is designed this way simply so that one can hold it in the palm of the trail hand, which allows the golfer to get and maintain a single plane throughout the swing.

As stated before, some of the main differences between the engineering of the two different types of clubs have to do with rotation of the club head, and where the rotation of that club head takes place during the swing. A golf club engineered for the conventional swing <u>will</u> rotate on its own through the impact zone and a club engineered for the single plane swing <u>will not</u>.

To prove this, all one has to do is plumb bob a golf club, holding it with the finger and thumb at the end of the grip with the toe of the club facing away from you. In this position, simply swing the club back and forth like a pendulum. With a toe-weighted club, you will notice that the toe of the club will open as the club goes back, and close as it comes forward. When you perform the same test with a center-weighted club the toe will not open and close but stay square.

Without this rotation of the conventional club through the impact zone, the club head will open up when it impacts of the ball on most off-centered hits causing a fade or slice. The engineering of the conventional club to rotate on its own through the impact zone is one reason why they are referred to it as fault-fixing clubs.

The Golf Shaft

To best understand why the shafts are designed the way they are, we must first understand the different methodologies of the two types of golf swings as stated above. With that thought in mind, I will explain why the shafts need to have different torques.

When comes to a golf shaft, all lower or higher torque means is: how much twisting there is in the shaft. A low-torque shaft will have very little twist in it, while a higher torque golf shaft will twist more. A good test is to hold the grip in one hand and the club head in the other, then twist the club. The more twist that occurs, the more torque there is in the shaft. The torque for the shafts Natural Golf uses on all their irons in graphite is L-flex—3.9, A-flex—3.8, R-flex—3.8, S-flex—3.6., and for the graphite woods, L—5.1, A, R, & S—4.1

A low torque shaft should be at or below 4.1 torque for the driver and woods, and at or below 3.8 torque for the irons. A lot of shaft manufacturers tried to make a shaft with that low torque without changing the shaft's flex and for years this was a problem, until a company named Apache Golf manufactured a shaft that would meet the specific requirements needed for a single plane/square tracking swing.

For the single plane swing, Natural Golf has developed a center-weighted club head and a low torque shaft with a stiff tip that will allow it to stay square to the target line throughout the impact zone, but <u>without</u> changing its flex. This is what Apache Golf Co. was able to do for the single plane swing.

One of the most important properties of a square tracking/center-weighted club verses a conventional toe-weighted club can best be illustrated by a simple test. Take a normal grip on a conventional club and ground the club face against something that is solid (like a chair or desk leg) and simply push it forward, not letting the grip to twist, as if it were going down the target line. <u>Do not rotate your hands</u>. See pictures below.

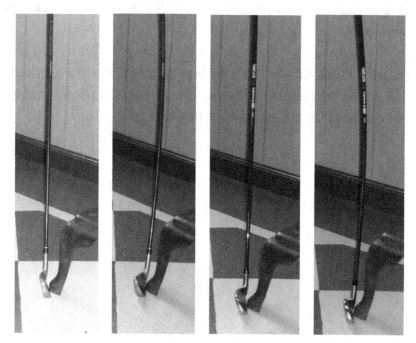

Higher Torque Shaft   **Lower Torque Shaft**
Toe-Weighted Club   **Center-Weighted Club**

The club face of the higher torque shaft has a tendency to open up under pressure. This is what happens when a golf ball is hit off centered using a toe-weighted club with a higher torque shaft that is swung in a single plane.

Repeat the same test with a low torque shaft/center-weighted club and you will see that the club face will not open but will stay square to the target line. As you can see, the center-weighted club does not need the extra toe weight to come to square throughout impact.

With the single plane swing, the clubface comes into the impact zone square and leaves square – this is what we call square tracking. With Square Tracking, a lower shaft torque, and center weighting of the club head, along with the non-tapered grip, the club will produce a straight ball flight even on most off-centered hits. This is what sets the single plane swing golf equipment apart from other golf equipment. Remember that the set-up will allow you to have a more reliable swing, **but the clubs must be able to do their part.**

Note: a lot of club manufacturers are beginning to bring the weight to the center of the club instead on the toe. This makes for a friendlier single plane club and gives a single plane golfer more options!

Chapter

13

PUTTING

Putting is probably the most important part of the game, not for the score but because of the way it makes us think! Just imagine if you three putt a green for a bogie you are so mad all you see is **"RED"** and that's all you can think about for the next three holds. Now on the other hand if you make a good one putt for a bogie you feel so good that you can't wait to get to the next tee. It's the same score!!!

When it comes to putting, to successfully make the putt in my opinion it takes 25 percent biomechanical skills and 150 percent confidence. If I have a student that tells me he can go on the green stand on his head and make putt, I simply reply stand on your head and make the putt. What I am putting in print is the best way I have found to assist most golfers in the making more putts. This is not - as stated before - the only way, it is simply a way. The grip use it to grip that will allow you to swing down the target line with the square blade to the target with as little movement as possible. I have found most of the movement of the body can be contributed to movement of the eyes. If one can keep their eyes still through the putting stroke, they have a great chance of keeping body motion to a bare minimum. An easy way to do this is after your setup is to focus on a spot on the ground directly behind a ball at close to the ball is you can get and focus only on it. You have done everything you can do to make a correct setup before focusing on the spot so all is left to do is to keep your eyes focused on that spot have confidence in your stroke and simply stroke the ball to the target. When this is done correctly you should see a shadow or an image of that ball in your peripheral vision after the ball is rolling to the target.

If the target line is further outside the eyes, the putter blade will have an inside to square to inside line, or an arc to the path. If this is the setup you chose you must pay great attention to ball position and make it correct at all times. In this setup if ball position is behind the normal position at address, the blade of the putter will have a tendency to be open at impact and the putt will roll out side its line because of the face being open. If the position is slightly forward than its normal position, the ball will have a tendency to be pulled off line because the face of the putter at impact will be in a close position. If the arms are in a neutral position, the blade of the putter will move more on a pendulum stroke, and the blade of the putter will be square to the line longer. If the ball position is out of position while making a pendulum putt, the line remains the same the only thing will change is the speed of the putt, but only slightly.

Putting is an art, but is an art that can be learned. The first thing we must talk about is posture. Posture with the putter should allow the golfer to do some things. First to be comfortable and 2nd is to allow the golfer to practice some basic fundamentals and/or DRILLS. I can tell everyone to get into a good putting posture, half will, half will not and all will think their posture is the best. So get into your posture as long as you are in balance and comfortable and can be steady which will allow you to practice. The only thing I stress is in your balance. Even more so than in the full swing. The balance position is critical. Balance position in the balance setup should be in the arches of the feet and feel as though at this time they have roots. What is meant by this is putting is the most precision shot/stroke you will make in the game of golf so the foundation should be the most solid. Just remember not to get so solid that you cannot relax.

When making a good putt two things must be accomplished, the first is get the right line to the target and number two is to create the right speed for that putt. Of these two fundamentals, speed is the most important. With the correct line and wrong speed, the ball can be left way short away long creating a long second putt. With the correct speed and the wrong line it will be hard to have more than a two foot 2nd putt on a level green. When it comes to the line, the ball will only come off the putter 90 degrees from the face of the putter. The direction the putter is traveling will only change the speed not so much the line.

The most repeatable stroke for most golfers is a pendulum stroke; it allows you to keep the blade of the putter square to the target line more consistent. The fundamentals for pendulum stroke are that the arms should be relaxed and hanging below your shoulders, all your hands and arms do in a in the stroke is hold the putter, that's all just hold on to the putter! The shoulders make the putting stroke with no arm or wrist movement. The hands, wrist and arms are part of the small muscle group that can move very quickly. The way they move they can produce a lot of leverage which in turn can produce a lot of speed and power. Leverage, speed and power are not what you are trying to do when you are putting. On the other hand your back and sides are of the large muscles group, they move slow and are very powerful with a lot of precision. Doesn't it make since that if you are trying to make the most precision move in golf that you use the most precise muscles?

The best way to achieve this movement is to get in your putting posture with your arms hang in below your shoulders, place your fingertips lightly together. Now move your arms and hands to the rear leg, back to the forward leg, back to address position with equal light pressure on both fingers tips using only the back muscles. If there's more pressure on one hand or the other then you are pushing with one of the hands. There must be equal pressure with both hands throughout the complete stroke. When you can create this movement with equal pressure on the fingertips it is time to take your putter grip. With putter in hand repeat the movements above and observe the putter blade. When doing this movement the putter blade should never get out of square from the target line.

Although speed is more important than line, I will explain line first. By practicing line first, it will build the fundamentals one needs in order to practice speed. As I have stated many times practice with a purpose, practice with a goal, but most importantly, practice one thing at a time.

Putter Alignment Drill

With this in mind we focus strictly on the line of the putt. Have a straight line on the ground or on the floor, this can be a string or what I like to practice with is a grout line in ceramic tile, anything straight. This line will represent your target line. Assume you're putting stance with the face of the club 90 degrees from the target line. Rise the putter off the floor about 2in. Using only the shoulders and making the pendulum stroke move the putter head from setup position to the trail foot, then to the lead foot, all the time keeping the putter blade square to that target line. Do the above movement (drill), until the putter blade stays square to that line naturally. Do this drill without a golf ball. Only then will it be time to move on to the next drill.

PUTT
MUST PUTT DRILL

The Must Putt Drill

This drill is called the Must Putt Drill because the golfer **must** do three things or "start the drill over". These three things are: at all times keep the blade of the putter square to the target line, the putter must not touch the ball behind the ball your putting and while performing the pendulum stroke with the shoulders the putter blade must move forward until it gets between your eye site and the hole. Your body will not want to do either of these but if either one of these things don't happen "you must start over". After mastering the alignment drill start by placing six balls directly in line going to the hole leaving 4" of travel for your putter between balls. Place the first ball on the ground 1' to 1 ½' away from the target. Continue placing balls in a straight line away from the target leaving the approximate 4" travel for your putter. Start with the first ball make a pendulum stroke and stroke the ball in the hole. Move to the second and repeat, continue until all balls have been putted. Do not stop this drill unless one of the tasks you're trying to complete did not happen and that case replace all balls and start again. The Must Putt Drill will teach of great many fundamentals if only practice correctly. These fundamentals are how to keep the blade square to the line, how to control the backswing, how to accelerate through impact, how to swing down the target line and most importantly how to make putts inside 6' and lower your score. The first to drills do not have to be done on a putting green. As long as you have low-nit carpet you can place one square of bathroom tissue on the floor, it is the same size of a golf hole, place a quarter or make a black dot in the middle of the bathroom tissue and performed a drill to it. When able to accomplish the alignment drill and then the Must Putt Drill it will be time to move along to the third drill, which is the speed drill or what is better known as the lag putting drill.

The Lag Putt Drill

The best way to learn how to control the speed of a putt is 1st learn how long your normal putt would be. You can achieve this by taking three balls on a putting green. With all three balls on the green, (placed side by side) putt all without looking to see how far they will run. Continue in this drill until your balls start making small groups, now you're putting stroke is starting to repeat. Next, step off from the spot on the green from where you putted to that group of balls. This will be the distance for your normal non-restricted putting stroke. Using my normal putting distance as an illustration I will best be able to describe the remaining drill. My normal putting distance is six steps on a flat Bermuda green. The greens where you live may be faster or slower than the Bermuda greens here in northeastern Florida, and if this is so you may have to regulate the formula that I use. Do this by adding or subtracting the amount of backswing per step. Do not take long steps or shorts steps when gauging this, only use normal steps. When learning how to generate the correct speed in your putt one must not try to hit the ball hard or easy. This will only reduce the consistency of your putting speed in the actual game of golf. Try to use the same stroke that you learned in the Must Putt Drill only in increasing or decreasing the backswing. Using my normal distance of six steps I can putt the distance putt using a formula of, **"1 in. of backswing for every one step of role = speed"**. The way to practice this drill is to step off the distance between the ball and the target, (the hole) and putt the ball using the correct backswing that pertains to that putt, just as a lot of the Pros' do! Watch them on TV, they just make it looks smooth. Do this drill without been concern about the target line until the backswing and the speed of the putt get in sync. Only after you feel comfortable with this speed drill will it be time to start thinking about the correct target line. Next we learn how to read the putting line.

Reading the Putting Line

Always line up your putts from behind the ball and facing the target. In your mind, draw a line from your target to the ball. Pick a spot on the green approximately 1 to 1 1/2 feet in front of the ball on that target line. This is your aiming spot for it is easier to aim at a target closer than farther away.

Once you have acquired the aiming spot on the target line never take your site off that spot while approaching and addressing the ball. The reason is your perception of the spot from behind the ball and at address will be different. If you take your eyes off of that spot it will be very hard to find that spot upon addressing the ball. Next, address the ball while looking at that spot, place the club behind the ball and aim the aiming lines on the top of the putter through the middle of the ball to that spot. This will square your putter to the target line. Now that you have picked your line and you know the distance or speed all that is left is to let all the drills come together and stroke the ball down the target line with the correct speed and make the putt.

It is important to remember that once you have the correct alignment and the correct speed of the putt you must commit yourself to that putt and just let it happen. And this is the hardest part of learning how to play golf. Some learn and enjoy, most don't. This part is learning to trust it! After learning how to putt, the worst thing a golfer can do is not trust themselves. No matter how good a drill or a series of drills they have practiced, if there is no confidence and trust in them, they will not be consistent. I'm convinced that the only way one learn to trust your putting stroke is by making putts,

The Putter

Your putter is the most important club in your bag. What I mean by this is that you will use the putter more than any other club. For example, if you use your driver "in regulation" you will only use it 14 times, but if you putt "in regulation" you will have used the putter 36 times. So doesn't it make sense to have your putter adjusted to fit you? After you have achieved a repeatable putting stroke check to see if your putter fits you.

You will first need to get into the putting setup with a good balanced stance. Make sure that you are in a relaxed position and that your eyes are directly over the target line. Now, let your arms hang naturally from the shoulders. Remember to stay in a good relaxed posture and do not bend forward to get your head over the line. Instead, move your body into or away from the line, keeping the correct body posture until the eyes are over the target line. Have someone hand you a putter. Put the center of the putter blade on the target line under the eyes and, with your arms hanging naturally, put the putter handle loosely in your the hands without moving the putter head. Only then do you grip the putter.

The sole of the putter at address should be flat to the ground from toe to heel. If it isn't, the putter's lie angle is out of adjustment. Also, putter faces can have as much as 2 to 6 degrees of loft. This loft can add to the deflection of the ball away from the target line if the sole of your putter is not flat to the ground. If the toe of the club is pointing up, there is a good chance that your putter will hit the ball to the left (for a right-handed golfer), and conversely to the right for a right-handed golfer. A good rule of thumb is this—for each one degree of (a) incorrect angle in the face of the putter (that is, open or closed in relation to the target line), or (b) incorrect lie angle, the ball will have a tendency to roll to the right or left of the target line 3" on a 10' putt. You can adjust the blade angle to make it square to the target line; a professional club fitter can adjust the lie angle of your putter to fit your putting setup and stance.

Chapter
14

CHIPPING

When it comes to chipping there are various ways, none better than others. I'm not going to tell you one way is better than the other that is up to the individual. Whatever method you choose will work, as long you have the confidence in that method and have the patients to practice the technique that that method requires. Some may be using one club and adjusting their stroke to fit the shot they require, while others use two or three clubs and adjust the stroke with the club they choose to get their results. As for me I'm convinced that it is far easier to learn one stroke and change your equipment to get the various results needed. I have seen in my teaching that this method is easier to learn and when perfected the consistency will be far greater. With this in mind let me explain the chipping technique that I teach. Please bear in mind this is not the only way just my way, after all I am the one writing this book. So without any further ado I give you "Chipping".

Chipping - Green Side

Just as inputting, chipping is an art, an art that can be learned. It can be learned by having the right knowledge, confidence and technique with a lot of practice. Knowledge comes from learning a technique and then having the confidence that if you practice it the right way, long enough, it would develop into the art you're seeking. There are many different ways chipping just as there are many different ways and play in the game of golf. I'm not about to say this is the only way, it is simply a way that I have been taught and that I know works. Some players take one club and chip with it no matter where they are or whatever the conditions they are in. This may work for the best golfers in the world, but for someone who cannot spend their life on or around the practice green I think they may want to consider the below technique, in the below technique you have only one stroke and change clubs for different situations. I'm a firm believer that if a golfer can execute a movement, then by changing clubs change the results - would it be easier to get the consistent results?

Just like in putting and pitching, Chip shots are precision movements. You will note in this chapter that I've started using the term "stroke". The reasons are – for most golfers, the stroke - not the swing is the most precise movement they can make. These strokes are made mostly by an upper body motion. The legs and waist only supports that movement.

When learning the art of chipping, three steps must be taken. The first is learning the correct setup, the second is learning a technique, and last but definitely not least - is gaining the confidence that will allow the setup and the technique to work consistently.

When it comes to the approach game, a good rule of thumb is this – the closer you are to the green, the more weight you put on the lead foot and the quieter the lower body. This helps you to hit the ball with a descending stroke; that descending stroke allows the club head to move through the grass more freely.

During my schools are lessons some of my students ask, "Do I have a favorite club when I am chipping?" The answer is no. When I am close to the green, I use a chipping setup, technique, and formula (which I will explain later) that lets me get the ball close to the flag every time. By changing clubs, you change the distance that the ball rolls; by changing the length of the backswing will change the distance the ball will fly. Using this method it makes chipping a lot less complicated because you do not have to change the tempo or rhythm using this technique simply change clubs.

If you will start using this same setup, technique, and formula for club selection, your ball also will end up close to the flag. It is important to note that when you are chipping from around the green, the target that you are trying to hit is not the flag, but a point on the green where the ball is to land. Always aim for a point about three feet into the green with every chip shot, no matter how far from the green the ball is, and no matter what club you are using. Your hands must be in the same position in your stance with all clubs and shots. The only variable will be your club selection, which is predicated on the distance you want the ball to fly and/or roll. How would you like to be able to learn one chipping technique and by doing so having learned all the chips shots? This is how it is done!

The Chipping Setup

When setting up for a chip, the shoulders should be in line with the target line. The feet should be parallel to each other but in an open position to the target line. This open position of the feet will allow the upper body a free range of motion with little if any lower body movement as you make the stroke. The feet should be between 4 and 6 in. apart with the majority of your weight on the lead foot (actually about 90%, remember you are very close to the green).Always maintain this weight on the lead foot throughout the stroke. By doing this and establishing the correct shaft angle at setup, you can control the loft and trajectory of that shot through a descending stroke. The ball should be in line with the trail foot approximately 1 ft. away from your trail toe and the clubface should be square to the target line. This setup will be the only time your head will be over or slightly in front of the ball position. See picture below.

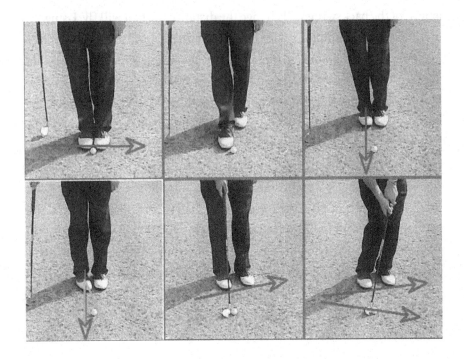

In chipping, it is very important to maintain the same loft on the face of the club throughout the stroke. I find that most golfers who have difficulty doing this are not setting the lead wrist in the proper position at address. When this happens, the wrist will break down and the club will not be able to maintain the same loft throughout the stroke. The trajectory and distance will therefore be inconsistent. The best way I know of to avoid this is to maintain a firm lead wrist.

For the lead hand, I recommend starting with the single plane swing (see picture "A" below).

(See Single Plane Grip).

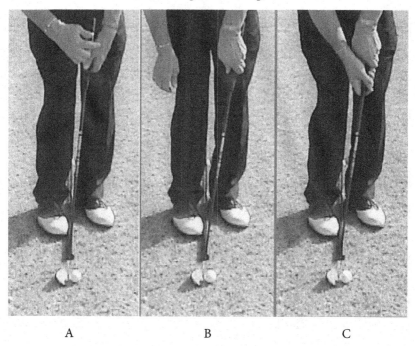

| A | B | C |

Next, rotate the lead hand (only the lead hand) around the grip toward the center of your body far enough so that all four knuckles will be at a 90-degree angle from the target line (in other words, all four knuckles will be facing away from you). See picture "B" above. Rotating the lead hand into this position at address will have the tendency to lock the lead wrist so that it will not break down through impact, and will set the correct angle of the club shaft.

The trail hand grip is in the palm and in line with the face of the club. What is meant by "in line with" is that the palm is aimed at the target (just as the face of the club). In this position, the lifeline of the trail hand will be on top of the lead thumb, in line with the clubface, and aimed at the target. See picture "C" above. Next, allow the lead arm to hang below the shoulder, which will place the hands in front of the lead thigh. The handle of the club will now be pointed outside the lead shoulder and in a single plane with the trail arm. This will produce the right shaft angle which, along with the weight on the lead foot, will produce the descending stroke.

The Chipping Technique

CHIP

Using this setup, let the upper body move in a pendulum or putting stroke, matching the length of the backswing to the desired flight of the ball to that point just three feet into the green (the primary target), not to the flag. The flag becomes only a secondary target, not the primary one. If you do not hit the primary target, you cannot consistently control the distance or speed of the ball.

The best way to achieve this technique is to use the same motion used in putting, the pendulum or putting stroke. As stated in chapter 14, (Putting) the best way to train yourself is, to get into your setup without a club, placing your fingertips lightly together. Now move your arms and hands to the rear leg, then back to address position with equal light pressure on both fingers tips. If there's more pressure on one hand or the other then you are pushing with one of the hands and not making the correct chipping stroke. There must be equal pressure with both hands throughout the complete movement. When you can create this movement with equal pressure on the fingertips, it is time to take your grip. With club in hand, repeat the above movements and observe the golf club. When doing this movement, the face of the golf club should never get out of square with the target line. To help you do this, draw an arrow on the face of the club with a marking pen as seen in picture below.

The final step in making the chip shot is to take the club back on the target line, keeping your swing path, target line and the arrow on the face of the club in alignment as you make the stroke. All that remains is to learn how to adjust the backswing with each club to get the desired ball flight! Remember the club you choose will give you the roll and the back swing you choose will give you the ball flight. Together these two things make up the chipping stroke.

Chipping Drill – Greenside

First, start by placing two tees on the green about three feet apart three feet into the green; this will be your target. Place a ball anywhere off the green. Get into a chipping setup with the ball in the proper position. Using the chipping technique, stroke the ball with any club so that it hits the ground between the tees. Remember – the target is the spot between the tees. Repeat this drill until the ball hits the target 8 out of 10 times, then move to another spot off the green and repeat the drill. After completing this drill, repeat it with the other clubs. The length of the backswing will determine the flight of the ball, and the loft of the clubs will determine the roll. This drill is meant to be practiced on level ground.

Intangibles

When playing chip shots, you should always take into consideration some intangibles. These intangibles will be: ball position, landing area, and the green. You will have to make adjustments with clubs and strokes for each of these intangibles. Always start from the ball and work to the flag. Check to see if the lie of the ball is uphill, downhill, or even side hill. Is the landing area sloped into or away from you or uneven, or does the green break to one side, or maybe the roll will be uphill or downhill?

Try to think of it this way, the lie of the ball will affect the flight of the ball, the slope of the landing area will affect the first bounce of the ball; along with the slope of the green, this will affect the length of the roll. With experience, you will be able to adapt to these different circumstances and select the appropriate club to deal with the intangibles you face.

Chipping Formula

To select the appropriate club, use the following formula. Determine a point on the green three feet in from the fringe. Pace off the distance from the ball to that point (length of ball flight); next, pace off the distance from the point on the green to the flag (length of roll). You need both of these measurements. If the first measurement is 3 steps to the point on the green and the remaining measurement is 15 steps from the point on the green to the flag, you will divide the roll (the 15 steps) by the ball flight (3 steps), which will give you the number 5. Subtract the number 5 from 12 (this is an arbitrary number that I find works). That leaves the number 7, telling you that your club selection should be a 7-iron. Here's another example: say it is 4 steps from the ball to the landing spot on the green and 24 steps from that spot to the hole. Again, divide 4 into 24 = 6, subtract 6 from 12 to arrive at 6; the 6-iron is your club. Here it is in summary form:

Chipping Formula

Roll divided by Flight, Subtracted from Twelve = Club

Or,

#1 Ball flight =?

#2 Roll=?

#3 Divide flight into roll =?

#4 Subtract that number from 12 and that gives you the club to hit for that chip shot.

11=s/w, 10=p/w, 9=9iron, 8=8iron, etc., etc., etc.

Approach Chip Shots

"Bump and Run"

The main difference between the bump and run setup and the greenside chipping setup are the feet at address. The bump and run shot is a longer version of the greenside chip shots. The longer distance in the bump and run calls for certain adjustments in the setup. First, the feet should be wider apart for more stability – preferably, the distance between the feet should be the width of the hips, and the feet should be in the same open position as for the greenside chip shot. I have found it more desirable to take a shorter backswing and a more accelerated forward swing to achieve the desired distance and line. This can be achieved by relaxing the trail elbow in the backswing and let it straighten itself out in the forward swing. In chipping, just as in every other aspect of the game of golf, the club should be accelerating through impact to control the trajectory and the distance of the desired shot. Practice with this technique in various lines and conditions. You may find this is a very valuable shot with a large amount of versatility. As Mr. Harvey Penick once said; the lower the trajectory of a chip shot the more you can control the rollout, and I have found this to be true.

Chapter 15

PITCHING

Just as in chipping and putting, the pitch shot is more of a precision stroke. The pitch is where golfers will start their short game, so we have to start thinking in terms of precision shots. In precision shots, it's more about how far the ball will go with a given swing than how far we can make it go with that swing. In the precision shots (the short game), the less movement one can have in the lower body and still make the swing, the better. A good rule of thumb is this – the closer the shot is to the flag, the less the lower body should move, and the more the swing is made from the torso, shoulders, and arms.

Another point is that somewhere between 60 and 70 percent of all scoring is influenced by the short game, that is, on or around the greens. The golfer should of course focus on the distant target skills for the power game that sets up the short game, but lower scores are determined more by the short game, the precision shots. Just think, a 1 in. putt cost the same as a 300 yd. drive....one stroke. So why not get proficient at all the skill levels, the power game, the approach game, and the short game (pitching, chipping, and putting)? It takes less strain and athletic ability to play short game shots to their respective targets, but this is the part of the game the weekend golfer does not practice. On the other hand, this is the part of the game the pros and top amateurs practice the most. Improving your short game, the precision shots can lead to the fastest improvement in your scoring!

151

I understand that there are physical limitations to the power game. Not everyone can or will be able to hit the 300 yd. drive, but anyone can pitch, chip, and putt. I cannot accept any excuse for not being proficient at the short game. It all comes down to is this: to have a proficient short game, one must have the right techniques, tweak them to fit one's own physical attributes, and then have the willpower to practice them correctly?

Let's start by learning the correct setup for pitching, then move to the correct technique.

Pitching Setup

The setup used in pitching is a combination of two setups that has been learned, (full swing and chipping). What I mean by this is although the position used in the upper body will be the same as the full swing, the lower half of the body will be in the position used in chipping.

Using a combination of the two setups as mentioned above will allow the shoulders to be square to the line while the hips, knees and feet will to be in an open position. This is to allow the shoulders to swing down the line while allowing the lower body to stay into a more of a stable position. This setup can be achieved by getting into the chipping setup, then move each foot 1 foot width to the side to open them. After the lower body has been set - rotate the upper body and allow the shoulders to become square to the target line.

At address the ball will be body-centered, not foot-centered. With the ball in this position it will appear (if seen from in front of the golfer) to be back in the stance, but in fact because of the upper body setup it will be in the center of the upper body. The feet should be flat to the ground and in an open stance relative to the target line; they will remain on the ground the entire swing. The inside width of the feet should be a little more than the distance between the outside of your shoulders. This will give the upper body freedom of movement throughout the swing and remain the stable stance.

More of your weight should be on the lead foot, say 65 to 70%, <u>and stay there throughout the complete swing</u>.

In the pitching setup and swing, because it is a precision swing and the feet are in an open position, the shoulders must be square to the target line at impact.

The grip will be the same as in the full swing, but lower on the handle of the club for better control of the shot and still in a single plane (See the chapter on grip).

Pitching Technique

In pitching, the set-up of the upper body and the path of the club will be in the same single plane, as in the full swing.

With the lower body in an open but stable stance, the upper body will be able to swing the club along the target line longer and more freely. The length of the backswing will determine the distance of the shot. Keep the same tempo and rhythm for all pitch shots (See chapter on Tempo and Rhythm). Remember that in precision shots it's more about how far the ball will go with a given swing instead of how far we can make it go with that swing.

In chipping and pitching, it is best to aim using a spot on the ground about two feet behind the ball, in line with the target, as a rear swing alignment point. Aligning your backswing to this spot will allow you to swing the club back on line. Take the club over top of that spot on the backswing and back over top of it on the forward swing. In precision shots, the ball will react to the face of the club, then the path of the club head, so if we can swing the club in the correct path with a square face we will have won half the battle. Now all you have to do is select the right length of backswing (which determines the speed of the club head) to give you the distance for the shot you want to make.

Backswing pitching drills

A   B   C

PITCH

Without a ball, practice backswings to the following three positions, remembering never to stop any forward swing – let the swing stop itself. Try to keep the <u>tip</u> of the handle in the middle your chest when swinging.

This will insure the proper shoulder turn. Too many golfers try to make the pitch shot using only the arms. It is an upper body swing - not an arm swing.

"A" position – Using only the upper body, swing the club back until the hands are just about to your trail pocket keeping the tip of the handle in the middle your chest. This will be called the "A" position.

"B" position – Again, using only the upper body, swing the club back until the hands are just about to your waist keeping the tip of the handle in the middle your chest. This will be called the "B" position. Keep the same rhythm.

"C" position – Once again using only the upper body, swing the club back until the hands are just about to your shoulders keeping the tip of the handle in the middle your chest. This will be called the "C" position. Keep the same rhythm.

Note, the tip of the handle of the club should be in the middle of the chest during the swing but not pointed at the chest - allow the risk to work freely.

Next, repeat the A, B, and C backswings with a ball and with all the clubs on the chart below until the distances are consistent. (You may have to do the drills three or four times to accomplish this.) Record these distances on the chart.

Pitching Chart

	A	B	C		A	B	C
l/w				l/w			
s/w				s/w			
g/w				g/w			
p/w				p/w			
9/iron				9/iron			
8/iron				8/iron			
7/iron				7/iron			
6/iron				6/iron			
5/iron				5/iron			

I have inserted two pitching charts because the more you get comfortable with the pitching technique your distance will change. You may have to change charts several times before it becomes reliable and consistent.

16

SAND PLAY

How often have you heard, "Oh man" not in the sand again! This usually comes from an inexperienced or a high-handicap golfer. I must admit that when I started out to learn golf, I made that statement many times. Like most golfers, I feared the sand, for I knew that almost every time I had a sand shot I could count on two or three strokes just to get out. This is exactly why most golfers cringe at the thought of hitting into a sand trap. This being so, I set out to find out how to consistently get out of the sand, and after I became a teacher I needed to learn how to explain what I learned in simple terms. Just like anything else in golf, the more you put into your game the more you will get out of it, and so it is in your sand play. If you say you can't get out, you probably won't get out. Getting out is easy to learn if you go through certain steps.

Once I realized that the sand shot is just another shot in golf that requires a certain technique, it was easy to get over my fear and learn. As long as you apply yourself and perform certain drills, you can overcome your fear of sand and develop the confidence and technique required for the shot. The same mind frame I teach my students for their putting lessons is required when they hit a sand shot. If you think you cannot get out of the sand, in most cases you will not, but on the other hand if you're convinced you are a good sand player and can get out of the sand, in most cases you will. I have said many times throughout this book that after learning the setup and the required technique, the game of golf becomes a mental game; sand is just one part of that game. From this point on, say to yourself, "<u>I am a good sand player.</u>" Keep reminding yourself of this fact. After performing these sand drills, in the right order, you will become that "good sand player." Remember, <u>you will become a better sand player by thinking you are, rather than by thinking you are not.</u>

Before we get into the actual techniques used in sand shots, we must first explore the available clubs and why their engineering makes them right for that technique. Every sand wedge has on its bottom what is known as "bounce." This bounce assists the club in getting the ball out of the sand. Certain clubs have to be rotated to an open position to increase the bounce, while others are designed to be swung using a square clubface. The club in the left picture (below) is the creation of Mr. Moe Norman,(the Sandy). He designed the club to facilitate the use of the square tracking technique in the sand. The club on the right is more of a traditional sand wedge, but is also modified to facilitate the square tracking of the single plane swing, only with an open face. See chapter 6, Equipment.

 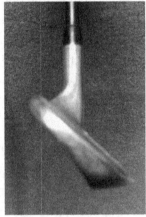

When learning sand play, you must decide which of the two sand wedges you will use. The first three drills will remain the same no matter which club you choose. But if you choose the more traditional design of the club designed for sand play, you need to move past the #3 drill and complete the remaining drill. So, let's get started!

Learn Your Ball Position

Before we can get started learning the sand drills, we must first check to see how we are swinging. This can be easily done by first simply drawing a straight line in the sand about 8 ft. long. Stand so that this line is in the middle of your stance with your feet an equal distance apart, then get into a golf stance, as shown above. Focusing only on the line, with your feet firmly planted in the sand, make a series of swings. After striking the sand the first time, move forward along the line approximately three to six inches and repeat the swing. Continue swinging and hitting the sand until you have used up the complete line. Check to see where you hit the sand in relation to that line; see if there is a pattern. If that pattern shows that you are hitting the sand more than 2 in. behind the line, it's a sign that you have little or no weight transfer.

If I had to pick the one fundamental that restricts most sand players from getting out of the sand, it would be the failure to transfer their weight. Most golfers who have trouble coming out of the sand will try to keep their weight in the center (or back of center) of their stance throughout the swing. To achieve the correct weight transfer, review the chapter on Drills, Weight Transfer.

After accomplishing the correct weight transfer, it will be time to start a series of sand drills so that you can become a good sand player.

Below is a series of drills that will help you to learn how to get out of a green-side sand trap. We will start with green-side bunkers, and later in this chapter we will cover fairway bunkers.

Greenside Bunkers

#1 Sand Drill

First, draw two lines in the sand, parallel to each other, approximately 1 ft. apart and 8 ft. long. A good tip it is to use the length of the grip as a gauge for setting the distance between the lines. Straddle the lines, making sure that they're in the middle of your stance.

Get into a good setup and make a golf swing, removing the sand between the lines. Just as before, step forward 3 to 6 inches after each swing and continue making your swing, each time removing the sand between the lines until you have traveled all 8 ft.

Repeat this drill until you can consistently remove the sand between the lines. The object of this drill is to contact the sand on the first line and have the club exit the sand on the second line. You must have the patience to complete this drill correctly before you move on to the next drill.

#2 Sand Drill

Again, draw the same two lines in the sand, only this time draw a third line in the middle of the first two. Place a golf ball just a little toward the target from the third (center) line and repeat Drill #1. In this case, just remove the sand between the two lines that are closer to the target. As in the #1 drill, move forward so as to remove new sand with each swing. After making three swings, removing new sand, make a fourth swing, this time removing both the new sand and the ball.

Repeat this pattern until the whole length of the lines has been used. Don't try to get ahead of yourself; have the patience to do the drill correctly.

#3 Sand Drill

After completing the line drills, it is time to complete the swing. To complete the swing, you must finish high. There has been a lot of confusion with what is meant by the term <u>finish high</u>. When golfers are instructed in finish high, too many think that the instructor is talking about their hands – this is not so. The term actually means finishing your body high. If you have not finished with your body high, you have not properly transferred your weight. If the body finishes high, then the hands and arms will also. See the above pictures. Both feet should remain flat in the sand throughout the swing.

If you have chosen to play a wedge like the Moe Norman Sandy, this will be as far as you need to go to learn the greenside bunker shot. If you have chosen to use a more traditional sand wedge, read on.

#4 Sand Drill

This sand drill will teach you the proper way to align your body to use the bounce of the club and not dig the ball out of the sand, but rather explode it out.

When learning to play out of the greenside bunker, you should learn how to open the clubface in order to utilize the bounce built into the bottom of the traditional sand wedge. Not all greenside bunker shots will require a sand wedge, but that's another lesson that we will cover later.

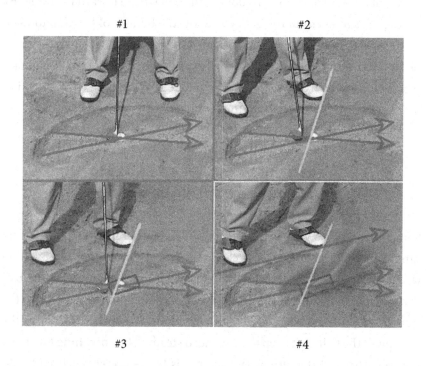

First, first take a normal single plane setup, square to the target.

Next, draw a half circle in the sand, (starting with your lead foot) with the ball in the middle. See #1 picture above.

Then, lay the club head on the sand and keep it there while you step around the circle (clockwise in the case of a right-handed golfer), until the line on the bottom of the club face points to the outside of your lead foot. See picture #2 above. In this position, you will be able to use the bounce of the sand wedge.

Next, draw a 6" rectangle box around the ball parallel to the line between your toes. See picture #3 above.

Then, with the line at the bottom of the club face still pointing to the outside of the lead foot, swing along your body line, taking the 6" box of sand out from under the ball. The swing path will be in the direction of the body, but because of the open clubface, the ball will go toward the target. By hitting the sand behind the ball, you allow the bounce of the club to work properly so that the club will be prevented from digging deep into the sand. This action of the club will lift the ball out of the sand without the clubface ever touching the ball. When this technique is applied, the ball direction will react to the clubface not to the swing path.

When not to use a sand wedge to get out a greenside bunker!

Sometimes you will find yourself in a bunker where there is little or no sand. When this happens, use a club with little bounce (such as a pitching wedge or a 9-iron), a club that will get the leading edge under the ball without much digging. If the sand is hard-packed and there is no lip to the trap, use a putter. If there is a small lip, chip it. But if there is a large lip, then pitch the ball; just keep the club head steady. The only thing I instruct the golfer to do differently with this shot is this – preset the weight onto the lead foot and keep it there throughout the complete swing, using only the upper body to make the swing.

The long bunker shot

Sometimes you will find yourself in a larger greenside bunker that requires that dreaded long bunker shot. In this case, use a less lofted club, like a pitching wedge or even a 9-iron, and make the same swing as if you were close to the green and had a sand wedge in hand.

The four rules when in the sand

#1 - get out! Or as I like to say - **anywhere green.**

#2 - get it on the putting green.

#3 - get it close to the hole.

#4 - get it in the hole.

Never give up #1 to try to achieve any of the other three.

Fairway Bunkers

Getting out of the fairway bunkers is easy for some, but for most it's one of the hardest shots in golf. This shot is only hard if you don't know the right techniques or don't have the confidence to use them. Confidence will come from learning the techniques and practicing them. The more you practice them the right way, the more confidence you will have in them when it comes time to play the shot. With that said, let's get started.

If you are an efficient golfer (a low-handicap golfer or a pro), adjust the single plane to fit the swing by gripping up or down on the club handle to adjust for the lie, place the ball back in your stance about an inch, and make sure to impact the ball first.

If you are not a low handicap golfer or a pro and you are having trouble getting out of the fairway bunker, the best way I know how to instruct you is this – take a club <u>two clubs longer</u> than you would have needed for the shot if taken from the fairway, <u>look at the top of the ball,</u> and make the swing <u>using only the upper body, keeping the legs quite still</u>. This way, you can become an efficient golfer when playing out of the fairway bunkers.

NOTE: Make sure when choosing a club that you can clear the lip of the sand that is in your target line. <u>Remember the #1 rule – get out!</u>

17

GOLF TIPS

Professional golfers have a strategy and a game plan for every course and every round of golf in a tournament. Most of the study for the tournament or their round was completed before they teed off. So take it from the professionals and have a strategy or a game plan for that round and course you will play. That strategy or game plan may be how you attack par five's, how to play the par three's or what you hit off the tee or maybe what clubs to put in your bag.

Most golfers think a full set of clubs is made up of 14 clubs, but this is not so. A full set of clubs may be 18 to 20 clubs. The USGA rules say you can only use 14 clubs on any given round, but not how many you have to choose from. The trick is to match your 14 clubs you carry in your bag to the course and conditions you will play. On a windy day you may need the shots to be low and on a rainy day with little wind you may need the shots to be high and soft. Same course different clubs, lower scores.

Below are some sayings and tips you may need to remember when playing or practicing, some you may have read in this book. Please try to only use one or two at a time!

~

Practice with a purpose, practice with a goal, but most of all,
Practice one thing at a time!

~

When learning a setup, it is a lot easier when you work from your feet up, not from your head down.

~

Stand tall to hit the ball, don't lose your balance or posture!

~

It has been said, and I agree, that 80% of shot making can be contributed to the setup. So if you can stop 80% of the flaws in your swing before you swing, isn't it worth learning?

~

Practice the drills slow to be able to make the swing fast. The slower you practice the drills the faster you will learn the SWING.

~

In the game of Golf there are basically two types of players. One is the Power player and the other is the Position player, let me explain.

First the Power Player – the power player is a player that hits the ball with a lot of speed and power. Driving the ball a long way, finding it and hitting it again. This player makes a full swing until he gets to close for his shortest irons, only then will they use his short game.

Next is the Position Player - the position player is a player that picks a target and hits to that target. This player may not be as long with his clubs as the Power player but usably more accurate with their play.

This is not to say that that a golfer can't and don't use parts of the other player's strategy but, it's is just that the way they play the game is their natural way of playing.

~

It is important to learn one drill before moving to the next.

~

The worst habit a golfer can have is the habit of, "Playing Swing instead of Playing Golf".

~

To play your best learn to play Golf is from "Green to Tee"!

~

Putting is the most important part of the game, not for the score but because of the way we think! If you three putt for a bogie you are so mad you see "RED" but if you one putt for a bogie you fill so good and can't wait to get to the next tee. It's the same score!!!

~

When practicing the drills with an impact bag, place the bag in front of the lead foot and make sure the arms are extended with the club face square to the target line when the club head contacts the bag.

~

Warm-up

Start by using a 7-iron and pick a target over 250 yd. away, hit short shots going at that target. Gradually get longer with your swing and distance until you are making a full swing still going at the target. Hit the club you will be hitting off the 1st tee (at the target). Chip, putt and then go and play. Do not try to hit too many balls before a round. Hit them after the round.

~

Learn how to play the par 5's

If you hit a long ball off the tee (250 yds. or more), play to the middle of the fairway, but if your tee ball is not as long it will better to play away from trouble such as a sand trap or a dog-leg. The par 5 is a 3 shot hole for most so don't play into the area that will make the next shot blind, always play the position that will give you the best change to have the largest landing area.

~

After learning the set-up and the swing motion, we must now learn how to put the club on the ball! See the Chapter on "Your Optics" This may sound a little funny but there are a lot of golfers that can hit the ball on the range but can't hit a ball on the course. After reviewing the chapter onHow to take your swing from the Driving Range to the golf course and Your Optics, and it does not help you will have, to approach it differently. My instruction to them is, buy a golfing net and a hitting mat. Hit balls off the mat into the net with all clubs making full swings. Next, make a target on the net with a piece of cloth about 8 inches wide in the middle running from the bottom to the top of the net so when the ball hits that spot it will make a loud sound. That sound will tell you that you have hit the ball in the middle of the target.

Get into the habit of listening for the sound of the hit, not trying to see it. Focus on it. Soon you will be able to hit it on the golf course.

~

If you need to gain the confidence in your swing and learn to be committed to the shot! The best way I know to achieve this is on the driving range. Have a practice session where you never hit at the same target two times in a row and never hit the same club two times in a row. Even if the shots are off line and/or you mis-hit them, go to the next target with another club. If you can't hit the ball doing this, it's time to go back to the net. If you are hitting the ball but it's off line, review the Chapter on target alignment.

~

Please do not try to accomplish too many things at a time, give yourself time to learn the one thing you are practicing then practice the next. Like hitting the ball, then hitting the ball at the target, then hitting the ball the right distance. If you can do it this way all you will have to learn next is, how to play the Short Game.

~

You don't need to know how to play golf in order to learn a good setup! But you will need to learn a good set-up, "TO PLAY GOOD GOLF"!

The four rules when in the sand

#1 - get out! Or as I like to say - **anywhere green.**

#2 - get it on the putting green.

#3 - get it close to the hole.

#4 - get it in the hole.

Never give up #1 to try to achieve any of the other three.

Your eyes are not the center of your single plane golf swing. They are only a focal point that keeps the center of your swing, which is your lead shoulder, in position. This eye position will also help you to look under the ball throughout your swing. A good drill to achieve this is to spray paint a line about 3 ft. long on the ground and another one about 4 inches to the rear of the first line. Place your ball on the 1st line and keep your eyes over the 2nd line as you hit balls off the 1st line. This will train you to keep your head back over your trail knee the way you were trained.

~

The essence of hitting a golf ball is to have the blade flat to the ground, square to the line moving down that line with enough accelerating club head speed to project the ball to its target.

Focus on execution, not results

One of the biggest flaws a golfer can make is to focus on results instead of concentrating on execution. If a golfer focuses on results and not on execution the results may or may not be accomplished. This is like what has been said as, putting the horse behind the cart. Until the golfer has practiced enough to make execution automatic, the focus should always come after execution. When this happens, the results the golfer is looking for will become more frequent.

To play the Game of Golf

To play the Game of Golf all one must know is, how to move a ball from one place to the other using the least amount of strokes.

This can be accomplished by knowing how to move the golf club from the pre-impact to the full extension as seen below! All the time making sure the club face remains square to the swing plane and using the maximum club head speed the golfer can control. This is all that matters! If this is simple for you, do not read any further, go out and play this Great Game and LOVE IT. If not, please move through this book slowly making sure you understand what you have read before going to the next. The worst thing I think one can do when trying to learn anything is, getting too anxious to know and moving too fast, ***"Slow down Please"***.

You cannot manipulate the golf swing

Since we were born we have tried to manipulate everything that we do, now you must realized you cannot manipulate the golf swing, you have to just let it happen. To get a proper golf swing you must think of two words. 1st word is "D R I L L", 2nd word is "S W I N G". They are not spelled the same, they are not pronounced the same and they don't have the same meaning. The DRILLS are not the SWING but only a small part of it, No one has ever learned the DRILLS by making a SWING but you can only learn the SWING by doing the DRILLS. To learn the SWING you must practice each drill *slowly*, until it becomes second nature then go to the next drill. This is the time to think about it; to make the SWING you must not think of the DRILLS, only the swing. If the swing is not there then go back to the DRILLS. To play the game of golf you cannot think about the golf swing, you must think "TARGET". If you have practiced the drills enough the right way you will have the confidence that the golf swing will be there so that you can focus on the TARGET.

Learn the DRILLS *slowly* to get to the SWING.

Practice the SWING to get the ball to the TARGET.

Think TARGET to play GOLF!

DRILLS

The Square Tracking & Impact Bag Timing Drill

Swinging Down the Line Drill

Grass Clipping

Swing Motion &Timing Drill

Shoulder Alignment Drills

Balance &Pos

Swinging Down the Line Drill

Wrist-cocking Drill

Motion to Resistant Drill

Hip-Slide Drill

The Impact Bag Drill

PUTTER Alignment Drill

The Must Putt Drill

The Lag Putt Drill

Chipping Drill - Green Side

Chipping Formula

Square Tracking and Swing Drills

Using the Black Dots

There are two words to remember; these words are "D R I L L S" and "S W I N G". These two words are not spelled the same, not pronounced the same, nor do they have the same meaning. No one has ever performed a drill by making a swing. But you can only build a swing by performing some drills. Do not confuse these two words. You have to do the drills very slowly in the conscious mind to build the memory in your subconscious mind. By performing the drills accurately in your conscious mind, you can transfer the learning to the subconscious. In other words, do the drills slowly so that you can make the swing fast.

The mind can and will play tricks on you if you don't pay attention. It will give you what you ask for; you have to be able to ask for the right things. What feels good to you may not be the correct things to achieve and the moves we are working on. More than likely if you are trying to change and the change feels well to you, it's usually wrong.

I keep hearing some instructors and players use the term muscle memory. Actually, there is no such thing as muscle memory. The only memory you have is found between your ears. The learning process in the brain is very unique. The way the brain learns biomechanics is through the conscious mind, "slowly". Think of it this way, if you were going to do your taxes yourself you would first find the correct form and record all information step-by-step, letter by letter, digit by digit until that form was correctly and completely filled out. There is no way you would put information on your tax form that was not correct, and you know why! Think of the golf swing in those terms. Each drill is a step, each position is a letter and each movement is a digit. Like I said before, your body will give you what you ask for, so you have to be able to ask correctly.

After reading this book and understanding the set up in the swing the drill in this chapter will reinforce all the lessons you have been taught. Your own evolution you may wish to do all the drills are simply choose the drill you need more reinforcement in and either case they are put in this book to help you succeed. I must reiterate what I've said throughout the complete book "please move slowly "and our repeat myself one last time, practice with a purpose practice with a goal and most importantly practice one thing at a time. Good luck can hit them straight!

~

The Square Tracking & Impact Bag Timing Drill

This drill is just as the title implies – it's a combination of drills condensed into one that teaches you how to square track, time the movements of your swing and head alignment. Just as in other drills, I combined several drills into one to simplify the movements and to allow you to learn faster. This drill – if done correctly – will teach you not only the above but also how to accelerate the club <u>through the impact zone,</u> which is vital when producing power.

This drill will be divided into five sub-drills with three steps in each. Only after learning those steps completely in each sub-drill will you move to the next. If you move slowly and hold each step for 10 sec. you will learn a lot faster.

Above are some of the aids needed to help with this drill, they are from left to right in the above picture: an impact bag, a jig I made for this drill, (from a straight board), and a rod about 3' long (I use a broken club shaft).

On the jig, I made some indicators such as, (a) a straight line from end to end through the middle (to indicate swing path and teach square tracking), (b) a small white spot (to indicate ball position), and (c) a white line 4" behind ball position, (to teach head position). If you don't have a jig, you can use any straight line with something to indicate ball position and head placement.

Before you start this drill we must first prepare your clubface. Draw an arrow in the center of the face of the club pointing down. See picture above. The arrow will help you see its direction and help keep it square when moving it through the drill.

The next thing we need to do is this, learn how to hold the club correctly with the lead arm. We position the club to have the tip of the lead forefinger and thumb on the shaft (below the handle). See grip, chapter 3. This will put the handle under the lead forearm when the club is held out straight in front of you. (See above picture)

Setup

The setup for your body in this drill is the same as in the full swing, but with the lead forearm and the hand placement as explained above. See chapter 3 setup. Lay the board on the ground with the impact bag at the lead end. Put the ball position in the middle of your stance. Position your head over the white line. Place the rod (the broken club shaft) in the ground about one inch from the outside of the lead foot.

Swinging Down the Line Drill

Just as in any drill – move slowly and hold each step in the static position for 10 seconds – let your body feel where you are asking it to be! I will repeat this throughout this drill for it is that important.

Sub-drill – 1

| Set-up | Step 1 | Step 2 |

After getting the set-up and holding the lead arm and club in a straight line, rotate them from the rotator cup. Move it to the rear thigh as in step 1. Look at the arrow in the face of the club and make sure that the club face stays square to the target line throughout this sub-drill. Next move the club to the impact bag using the same arm motion as in step 2 above.

Make sure to keep your head over the white line and also remember to hold each position for 10 seconds.

Sub-drill - 2

| Setup | Step 1 | Step 2 | Step 3 |

The second sub-drill has three movements. Now that you have completely learned the first two moves in drill – 1 we will move to drill - 2 and the third movement.

Continue doing the first two movements, only this time after completing Step 1, insert the movements demonstrated in Step 2 above. This movement is maintaining head positioned over your trail knee while moving the lead thigh to the rod. This move will place your spine angle in the correct position. After this new Step 2 has been mastered, move the club to the impact bag using the new spine angle and maintaining the feet flat on the ground. This will become Step 3. Look at the arrow in the face of the club and make sure that the club face stays square to the target line throughout this drill. Make sure to keep your head over the white line and also remember to hold each position for 10 seconds.

Sub-drill- 3

| Setup | Step 1 | Step 2 | Step 3 |

To perform this drill move the club to the trail hand making sure that the forefinger and thumb is on the shaft and the tip of the handle points to the lead shoulder, Make sure to keep it pointed at the lead shoulder all times while repeating the movements of drill – 2. When performing step three the shoulders will have to rotate around the spine to allow the club to impact the bag while maintaining the feet flat on the ground. Check and make sure that all the angles are correct. Look at the arrow in the face of the club and make sure that the club face stays square to the target line throughout this drill. Make sure to keep your head over the white line and also remember to hold each position for 10 seconds.

Sub-drill- 3

| Setup | Step 1 | Step 2 | Step 3 |

The first step of Drill - 3 is to place both hands on the handle, with the tips of the trail fingers still on the shaft and the end of the handle in line with the under arm of the lead forearm. Next, repeat the movements of drill – 2. Look at the arrow in the face of the club and make sure that the club face stays square to the target line throughout this drill. Make sure to keep your head over the white line maintaining the feet flat on the ground and also remember to hold each position for 10 seconds.

Sub-drill- 4

| Setup | Step 1 | Step 2 | Step 3 |

Drill – 4 is the same three steps in drill - 3 only you must allow the trail elbow to bend and the hands to go to your waistline. This will become the new movements to Step 1 position. Continue through the drill as in drill – 3 only rotate the shoulders forward as the lead knee goes to the rod maintaining the feet flat on the ground. You will notice at this time that your sternum will be facing the impact bag and you may noses that this position is the same as the number 4 timing position or what is known as full extension. . Look at the arrow in the face of the club and make sure that the club face stays square to the target line throughout this drill. Make sure to keep your head over the white line and hold each position for 10 seconds.

Sub-drill- 5,

| Setup | Step 1 | Step 2 | Step 3 |

Top of backswing   #3 Timing position   #4 Timing position

After you can take the drill to the waist and through to step 3, (in time) we can complete the drill. When going to step 1, now allow the trail elbow to move to the side and the shoulders to complete the backswing. This will become the new step 1 position. By looking at the picture above you will notice the new step 1 position is the top of the backswing. The step 2 position is the same as number 3 timing position and step 3 in the above picture is the same as the number 4 timing position or what is known as full extension. Look at the arrow in the face of the club and make sure that the club face stays square to the target line throughout this drill and the feet are still flat on the ground. Make sure to keep your head over the white line and also remember to hold each position for 10 seconds.

NOTE: *only after all the drills have been completed, does the movement of the swing gradually gain in speed until the correct tempo and rhythm has been achieved while maintaining the timing of the complete swing.*

At this time the Square Tracking and Swing drills will have been completed. Remember, anytime any drill goes to the #4 timing position, make sure that the arms are fully extended and in line with the spinal alignment. The arrow on the face of the club should be in line with the straight line on the floor, or the target line, when the club head impacts the impact bag or goes though the impact position!

~

Grass Clipping

Swing Motion &Timing Drill

When trying to learn the motions of a single plane swing, the fastest way is to perform what is called, Grass Clipping or the Swing Motion and Timing Drill. This drill is a continuing motion drill. If the drill is stopped for any reason, it should be started again from the beginning. As stated, I cannot teach feel, one can learn it, but it cannot be taught. With this in mind, all I can do is explain what needs to be done but only you (the golfer) can experience the sensation (feel). It is important to note that when doing this drill we will concentrate on only one part of the body at a time. For example, when we talk about an elbow for instance, try to focus only on that elbow and no other part of the body. When moving from one step of this drill to another, the focus will move to the next, but one must continue to allow the last step to complete itself. When this drill is done correctly, there will be a metamorphosis in the golf swing. What is meant by this is, when the drill is done correctly the motions learned by this drill when combine with the natural actions done of the rest of the body will produce the correct motions needed to perform the single plane swing.

There are some things one must know to perform the drill correctly. With the eyes open, most of the data that's get to the brain will be through the eyes. Once the eyes are closed, most of the data that goes to the brain will be through your other senses, (feel). With this in mind, we will be doing some moves with the eyes open, but most with the eyes closed.

To start the drill, take a lofted iron and get into the single plane setup.

Step One

After completing this setup and with the eyes open, swing the club back and forth down the target line far enough to get it wider than the power zone. Once this step has been completed, continue swinging the club and have it brush the grass both ways. While swinging the club, close the eyes and listen for the club head as it goes through the grass.

Step Two

With eyes closed and listening to the club head, have the sensation that the trail elbows is moving <u>past your back</u> in the backswing. You should have the sensation that the rear forearm is moving in a lateral line while staying close to the side. Make this move until it feels natural. See picture above.

Step Three

Again, while the eyes are closed and you are listening for the sound of the grass, allow your attention to go to the lead elbow. Focusing only on the lead elbow, have the sensation that the lead forearm is moving in a lateral line while staying close to the side and the lead elbow is moving past your back, the same as the trail elbow.

It is important that we do not stop one motion that we have completed to accomplish the next. We are building this drill step-by-step. Do these two motions until they become natural.

Step Four

Again, while the eyes are closed and listening for the sound of the grass, allow your attention to go to the lead hand. While allowing the elbows to continue working, push the lead hand away from the body in the backswing as far as it will go. In other words, in the backswing, try to extend the hand as far as it will go, away from the body until the arm gets parallel to the ground. With the hand in this position, point the thumbs away from the target line as if in a hitchhiking position. When this move has been accomplished, the lead hand will be pointing away from the target. The grip end of the shaft will be pointing at the target line. Do these three motions until they become natural. One of the added benefits of performing the drills with the eyes closed is at this position of the drill you will be able to feel the weight transfer to the trail side.

Step Five

Again, while the <u>eyes are closed and listening for the sound of the grass,</u> allow your attention to go to the trail hand. In the forward swing extend the hand as far as it will go away from the body until the arm gets parallel to the ground. When the arm gets parallel to the ground, push the hand away from body and have the sensation that you are pointing your trail index finger at the target. As stated before with your eyes closed you will be able to feel the weight transferring back to the lead side.

Step Six

Again while the <u>eyes are closed and listening for the sound of the grass,</u> allow your attention to go to the finish. To complete the finish, all one has to do is after step five has been completed, count three swings, then on the fourth swing, allows it to continue until it is a complete follow through to a relaxed finish.

See Chapter 4, #6 Timing Position

It is important to note that as we move through these motions, we are using the steps in the drill to create building blocks in the mind. <u>Do not stop</u> a motion in order to achieve the next in this series. If you cannot complete the next step without continuing the last one, then you have not completely learned the previous motion. Go back and practice until you can!

Some things one will notice when doing this drill is how much the shoulders have turned and how little the waist turns without even trying. Also, how the feet will stay on the ground until after step five is completed and how steady the spinal column stays.

Only after this drill has been completed with the eyes closed, can the last step be done! The last step is to open the eyes and complete the drill again, checking alignments and movements.

Shoulder Alignment Drills

The main reason for pulling or pushing ball flight is shoulder alignment at impact. The fastest way to correct this misalignment is to go back to the setup. With the single plane swing being an upper body swing, the shoulders will rotate more in the forward swing than the lower body so we have to adjust for it in our setup, (see chapter 5). This being so, the shoulders must be in the correct position at setup. This is how to setup and how to check it!

Make an alignment jig using two clubs and here is how it's done. First lay two clubs on the ground; the toes facing you with the grips facing the target and the club further away from you on the target line. Align the clubs so the bottom of the grip is touching and the club heads are touching from the toe of one to the heel of the other, (see picture below). At address, the body should be aligned to the club on the target line. The shoulders should be aligned tithe club shaft from inside to outside; this will set your shoulders and spinal alignment to the proper setup position.

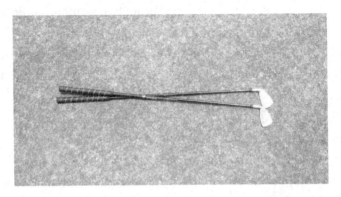

Next, assume your natural setup position making sure you have the correct "y" angle in your arms and club with the proper ball position with your feet the same distance from the club that is square to the target line. Let the lead hand remained stationary and place the palm of the trail hand on the rear of your trail buttocks. Making sure you maintain the straight lead arm and the club alignment, let your trail hand move down the back of your trail leg, (not the side of the leg, the back of it) about half way to the knee or until your shoulders are in line with the 2nd club. This will move your shoulders into the correct alignment position, remember where it is, feel it and practice it! Remove the trail hand from behind the trail leg; do not rotate that hand; reached underneath the handle of the club with the palm of your hand pointing up and get the correct grip.

Some students ask, "how far should the hand go down the back of the leg"? I answer this way; as far as it needs to get the shoulders aligned with the clubs. Again, remember where it is, feel it and practice it! This is a drill so move slowly.

~

Balance &Pos

Drill: once achieving the #1 timing position, move from the setup position to the #1 timing positions slowly and hold it in a static position. The best way to achieve this movement is to get in your setup without a club and place your fingertips lightly together. Now move your arms and hands to the rear leg, back to address position with equal light pressure on both fingers tips. If there's more pressure on one hand or the other then you are pushing with one of the hands and not making the one peace takeaway. There must be equal pressure with both hands throughout the complete movement. When you can create this movement with equal pressure on the fingertips, it is time to take your grip. With club in hand, repeat the movements above and observe the golf club. When doing this movement, the golf club should never get out of square from the target line. To help in keeping it straight, draw an arrow on the face of the club with a marking pen. See picture below.

Go from #1 to #2 back to #1, then repeat slowly and let your body get a since of these positions. You may also want to do this drill in front of a full-length mirror.

Swinging Down the Line Drill

In this drill, you will be hitting balls off a hitting mat. Place the ball about 6" behind the rubber tee and on the target line - make sure to hit the ball and then the tee. Next, move the ball to 8" behind the tee and again hit both the ball and the tee. Lastly, move the ball 12" back and hit them. If you can hit both the ball and tee at 12" you will be swinging down the line.

Wrist-cocking Drill

Perform this drill and you can learn where the arms go in the backswing, how to maintain a straight lead arm, and where the trail elbow is positioned.

Get into your setup. Maintaining the "y" angle of the arms, from the wrists only bend them to the full cocked position. At this time, the club shaft will be pointed away from you at a 45-degree angle, but still in line as the lead forearm. Keeping the wrists cocked, rotate the shoulders to the trailside – allowing the trail elbow to bend to the trail side until the lead arm is parallel to the ground and the club handle is pointing at the target line. In this position and with the club shaft pointing at the target line, you will be in a single plane.

Motion to Resistant Drill

Because as I've said many times I cannot teach feel, I can only explain it. With that in mind if you are having trouble completing your backswing please try this motion to resistant drill.

In order to achieve the correct position at the top of the backswing, (remember everyone's backswing is different) get into a stable stance. Next, interlace fingers and point elbows away from each other. Rotate hands until the thumbs of both hands are pointed toward your chest and lay them lightly on your chest. Assume a natural golf setup without a club and with the correct spine angle. As seen in the picture below, Set-up. Place a ball on ground in the correct ball position; never take your eyes off the ball. Rotate the shoulders to your full backswing keeping the thumbs on your chest and arms straight. At the top of your backswing there will be a tight feeling in the lead side and the lead foot will be on the ground, heel to toe.

Set-up

Hip-Slide Drill

If you are having difficulty getting the lower body to the #4 timing position this drill will help. In order to achieve the correct motion to the #4 timing position with the lower body, the hip slide must be achieved. This drill is a continuation of the backswing drill. After the backswing has been completed and after you have rotated the shoulders into the backswing, keeping the thumbs on your chest and arms straight. Let the lead knee relax and move over top of the little toe on the lead side, make sure the trail leg stays straight but not locked in joint, but relaxed. Halfway through, the knee movement starts rotating the shoulders forward to where the trail elbow points to the trail foot, keeping the arms straight and the thumbs on your chest. When this drill is done correctly, you will have a slight pull on the inseam of the trail leg and your head will lower, but stay behind the ball. Both feet should remain on the ground throughout this exercise. Return to the original set up position and repeat both drills together, slowly (see picture above). Do the drills with eyes open and closed.

"WARNING "This drill should be practiced enough to become 2nd nature. Do not think about this movement when swinging, let it happen! If it doesn't happen, then you have not done it enough! If you think about the drill or the movement while swinging, the shot will have a tendency to go off line to the right for a right handed golfer.

If you think about this drill when swinging, the trail shoulder will start moving around the body instead of descending to the trail foot, making the ball to go right for a right handed golfer, left for a lefty. Make sure the trail elbow points to the trail foot. If you start the forward swing with the shoulders, this will happen by itself. See Chapter 7, Sequence of the Swing.

The Impact Bag Drill/The #4 Timing Position

Using an impact bag, make a straight line on the floor or ground that will be your target line. Place the bag outside the lead foot and on that target line. With an arrow on the face of the club, slowly swing the golf club to the trail foot then back to the bag making sure the arrow stays pointed to and in line with the target line. Next go to the #2 timing position back to the bag making sure the arrow stays pointed to and in line with the target line. Next, go to the top of the swing, back to the bag making sure the lead arm and club are in line when the club contacts the bag and also making sure the arrow stays pointed to and in line with the Target line. . Slowly repeat this drill until it is in time, and then gradually start building up the tempo and rhythm of the swing.

Note, this will be a good time to see if the Hip-Slide Drill is working!

Putting Drills

PUTTER Alignment Drill

With this in mind, we focus strictly on the line of the putt work. Have a straight line on the ground or on the floor; this can be a string, drawn on the floor, or what I like to practice with is a grout line in ceramic tile. Do the above movement (drill), until the putter blade stay square to that line naturally. Do this drill without a golf ball. Only then will it be time to move on to the next drill.

The Must Putt Drill

This Drill is called the Must Putt Drill because the golfer must do "three things" or start the drill over. These three things are: keep the blade of the putter square to the target line at all times, the blade of a putter must not touch the ball behind the ball you are putting, and while performing the pendulum stroke with the shoulders the putter blade must move forward until it gets between your site and the hole. Your body will not want to do either of these, but if either one of these three things don't happen, you must start over. After mastering the alignment drill, start out by placing six balls directly in line going to the hole leaving 4 in. of travel for your putter between balls. Place the first ball on the ground possibly 1 to 1 ½' away from the target. Continue placing balls in a straight line away from the target leaving approximately 4 in. of travel for your putter blade. Start with the first ball making a pendulum stroke and stroke the ball in the hole. Move to the second and repeat, continue until all balls have been putted. Do not stop this drill unless one of the tasks you're trying to complete did not happen. In that case, replace all balls and start again. The Must Putt Drill will teach many great fundamentals if only practice correctly. These fundamentals are how to keep the blade square to the line, how to control the backswing, how to accelerate through impact, how to swing down the target line and most importantly how to make putts and lower your score. The first two drills do not have to be done on a putting green. As long as you have low nit carpet, you can place one square of bathroom tissue on the floor, it is the same width of a golf hole, place a quarter or make a black dot in the middle of the bathroom tissue and perform a drill with it. When able to accomplish the alignment drill and then the Must Putt Drill, it will be time to move along to the third drill, which is the speed drill or what is better known as the lag putting drill, (See Chapter 15)

The Lag Putt Drill

The best way to learn how to control the speed of a putt is learn how long your normal putt will be first. You can achieve this by taking three balls on a putting green. With all three balls on the green, (placed side by side) putt all without looking to see how far they will run. Continue this drill until your balls start making a small group. Next, step off from the spot on the green where you putted to that group of balls. This will be the distance for your normal non-restricted putting stroke. Using my normal putting distance as an illustration, I can best describe the remaining drill. My normal putting distance is six steps on a flat Bermuda green. The Greens where you live may be faster or slower than the Bermuda greens here in northeastern Florida, so you may have to regulate the formula that I use. Do this by adding or subtracting the amount of backswing per step. Do not take long steps or shorts steps when gauging this, only use normal steps. When learning how to generate the correct speed in your putt one must not try to hit the ball hard or easy. This will only reduce the consistency of your putting speed in the actual game of golf. Try to use the same stroke that you learned in the Must Putt Drill, only in increasing or decreasing the backswing. Using my normal distance of six steps I can putt any distance using a formula of 1 in. of backswing for every one step of role = speed. The way to practice this drill is to step off the distance between the ball and the target, (hole) and putt the ball using the correct backswing that pertains to that putt. Do this drill without being concerned about the target line until the backswing and the speed of the putt are in sync. Only after you feel comfortable with this speed drill will it be time to start thinking about the correct target line. Next, we learn how to read the putting line. Always line up your putts from behind the ball and facing the target. In your mind draw a line from your target to the ball. Pick a spot on the green approximately 1' to 1 1/2' feet in front of the ball on that target line. This is your aiming spot. Once you have acquired the aiming spot on the target line, never take your site off that spot while approaching and addressing the ball. The reason behind this is your perception of the spot from behind the ball and at address will be different. If you take your eyes off of that spot it will be very hard to find that spot upon addressing the ball. Next, address the ball while looking at that spot, place the club behind the ball and aim the aiming lines on the top of the putter through the middle of the ball to that spot. This will square your putter to the target line. Now that you have picked your line and you know the distance or speed, all which is left is to let all the drills come together and stroke the ball down the target line with the correct speed and make the putt. It is important to remember that once you have the correct alignment and the correct speed of the putt, you must commit yourself to that putt and just let it happen. After learning how to putt, the worst thing a golfer can do is not trust them. No matter how good a drill or a series of drills they have practiced, if there is no confidence and trust in them, they will not be consistent.

~

Chipping

Chipping Drill - Green Side

First, start by placing two tees on the green about 3 feet apart onto the green; this will be the target. Place a ball anywhere off the green. Get into a chipping setup with the ball in the right ball position. Using the right chipping setup and technique, (see chapter 16) stroke the ball with any club so in its flight it hits the ground between the tees. Remember, the target is the tee. Repeat this drill until the ball hits the target 8 out of 10 times then move to another spot and repeat the drill. After this drill has been completed, repeat the same drill with the others clubs. The backswing must determine the flight and the lofts of the clubs will determine the roll. This drill is meant to be practiced on level ground.

~

After learning the setup and the swing motion, we must now learn how to put the club on the ball! This may sound a little funny but there are a lot of golfers that can hit the ball on the range but can't hit a ball on the course.

After reviewing the chapter on *How to Take Your Swing from the Driving Range to the Golf Course*, (chapter 10) and *Your Optics*, (chapter 9) and it does not help then we must take it another way. Some have told me they can hit golf balls good everywhere but the golf course. I tell them to buy a golfing net and hitting mat. Make a target on the net with a piece of cloth or whatever; something to focus on. Always hit at the target and soon you will be able to hit it on the course.

~

Square Tracking and Swing Drills

Prepare for these drills by having a straight line on the floor or ground. Mark the clubface with an arrow in the center of the face pointing it to the bottom. Place an impact bag outside the lead foot with the line on the floor going into the middle of the bag. Get into the single plane stance, (see Setup). Always grip the club with the index finger and thumb on the shaft and the remainder of the hand on the grip. With the feet square to the line, stand far enough away to let the arrow on the clubface to be above and in line with the line on the floor.

Lead Arm Drill

This will be a two-step drill at first then move to a three-step drill. To do the two-step drill get into the correct setup, see above. After getting the lead handgrip, place the end of the grip under the lead forearm making a straight line from shoulder to club head. Next, set the club in the center of the stance, move the club from only the shoulder, from the setup position to just outside the trail leg; this is the #1 position. Next, move the club head to the impact bag in front of the lead foot; this will be the #2 position, always keeping the arrow and line on the floor in line with each other. Note: only the arm is moving, the body doesn't move.

Next, we go to the three-step drill. In the three-step drill, after the #1 position has been achieved, hold that position in place and relax the lead knee and let it move to over the top of the lead little toe. This position will become the #2 position and the old #2 will become the new #3. Move next to the new #3 position. Always keep the arrow and line on the floor in line with each other. Note: only the arm is moving in this drill, the body does not move!

After accomplishing the individual steps to the three-step drill and are confident we know how the produced them will be time to move on. The next phase to the three-step drill is to make all three movements in a continuous motion. These steps of the drills will be continuous movements. These movements will be slightly overlapping. This means, before the #1 position had been, acquired the lead knee should be moving to the #2 position. Before the #2 position is completely achieved, the arm should be moving to the #3. In this particular phase of the drill, the body will move forward to anticipate and support the movement of the arms, but there is no body movement going to the number one position. When done correctly in this phase of the drill, you will have a sensation that the lower body will be pulling the arm forward.

Trail Arm Drill

In this drill we substitute the lead arm for the trail arm. Just as in the lead arm drill the index finger and thumb is on the shaft and the remaining part of the hand on the grip. After acquiring the palm grip and single plane with the trail hand, continue with the lead arm drill. Repeat the two-step drill, then the three-step drill. The trail arm drill is the same as the lead arm drill with the exception of where the handle of the club is pointed. The handle of the club should be pointed to the lead shoulder and remain pointing there throughout the complete drill.

Two Arm Drill

Keeping the trail hand on the grip with the index finger and thumb on the shaft, position the lead hand on to the grip in the proper placement, See single plane grip. The handle of the club should be pointing at the lead shoulder. Repeat the two-step drill, next the three-step drill using of both arms, remember in the one and the two-step portions of this drill only the shoulders and arms are moving; the body does not start to move until you start the three-step portion of this drill. Repeat this drill until it becomes natural.

Just as stated before, the entire three step drills on a continuous movement and will be slightly overlapping in their movements. In this particular phase of the drill the body will move forward to support and anticipate the movement of the shoulder then arms but never to the drive the swing. When done correctly," in this phase of the drill" you will have a sensation that the lower body will be pulling the arms forward. Repeat this drill until it becomes natural.

Next, after reaching the #1 drill position, relax the trail elbow and let it bend just a little. Next, do the same drill except let the trail elbow relax a little more, then a little more, then a little more until the backswing is parallel to the ground. Complete the drill all the way to the #3 timing position. At this time hold the arms at parallel to the ground then relax the lead wrist and let it go to a full wrist-cock. Hold this position and get the sensation of what a full 90-degree wrist-cock feels like. Repeat this drill until it becomes natural.

Continue the swing until the backswing has been completed, then go to #4 timing position, then back to the top of the back swing back to the #4 timing position, "SLOWLY". Repeat this drill until it becomes natural.

NOTE: *only after all the drills have been completed, does the movement of the swing gradually gain in speed until the correct tempo and rhythm has been achieved while maintaining the timing of the complete swing.*

At this time theSquare Tracking and Swing drills will have been completed. Remember, anytime any drill goes to the #4 timing position, make sure that the arms are fully extended and in line with the spinal alignment. The arrow on the face of the club should be in line with the straight line on the floor, or the target line, when the club head impacts the impact bag or goes though the impact position!

Using the Black Dots

When placing the hands correctly on the handle of the club, we can use our hands and wrists as reference points. Because the wrists are in the un-cocked position at address, and in the cock position at the top of the backswing, we can use that knowledge to align the placement of the hands on the club. One can do this by using our knowledge of our own wrists and hands.

Holding your left hand as described in the picture below, notice the small cavity (indicated by the pointer) just between the base of the thumb and the inside wrist bone.

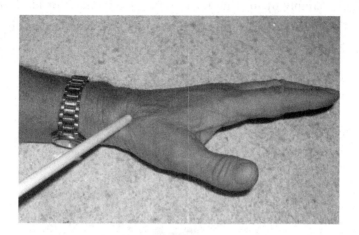

This cavity is what's known as the pill box. This pill box is what allows your hands to have the motion that is called cocking or un-cocking. To identify this pill box, to run your finger along the thumb towards the wrist until it drops into the cavity, which is in line with that thumb. Without this cavity (pillbox), the movement of the wrist in a hammering movement, (single plane swing) could not happen.

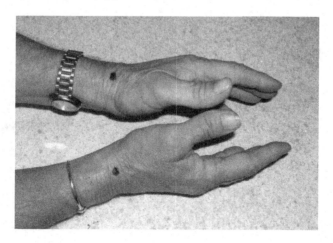

See the above picture. Note the identification mark I've made in the middle of each hand's snuff box. We can now use our eyes to align our hands on the handle of the club to make sure that they are in the correct position at address, simply by looking for the marks. The mark or black dot on the lead hand should be in line with the top of the handle at address (see picture below).

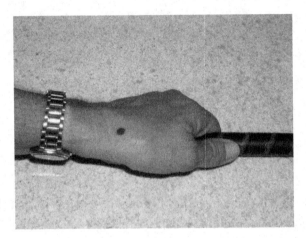

In other words, if there was a dowel rod starting at the wrist that passed through the dot and through to the handle of the club, that dowel rod would be pointing down through the handle.

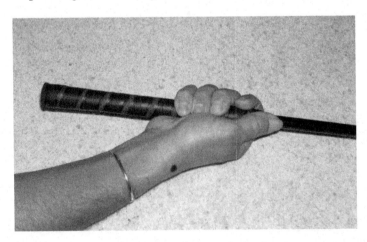

Now see the above picture. The dot on the trail hand will be behind the grip at address. Using the same analogy as in the lead grip, if a dowel rod starting at the wrist were to pass through the dot on the trail hand and then through to the handle of the club, that dowel rod will be pointing to the target.

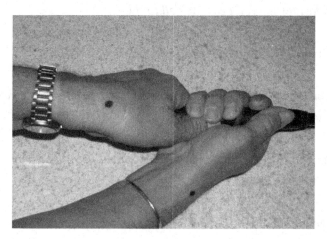

The picture above now shows the correct position of both hands. As one can see by this illustration, in the single plane palm grip, the palms of the hands do not appear to face each other. The reason for this is that each hand has a separate job to do in the single plane swing. The lead hand will guide the face of the club through impact, while the trail hand will produce the power in the swing.

Chipping

To determine your club selection use the following formula. Determine a spot on the green three feet in from the fringe. Pace off the distance from the ball to the spot and then on to the pin. Say it is 4 yards to the spot and the remaining is 16 yds. Divide (the roll), 16 yards by the spot yardage 4 and that will be 4. Subtract 4 from the operative number 12. That leaves 8 telling you that your club selection should be an 8 iron. *Say it is a total of*

30 yards from the ball to the hole with the spot being 4 yards from the ball. Again divide 4 into 24 = 6, 12 – 6 = 6, 6 iron is your club.

Chipping Formula

#1 Take how far you need the ball to fly.

#2 divide that into how far you need the ball to roll.

*#3 Take that number subtract it from the # **12** and this gives you the club to hit.*

*EX, if the ball flies 4 yards, then rolls 16 yards, you divided **16 by 4 = 4.** Subtract 4 from 12 = 8*

***8iron is your club.** But remember to hit the spot (on the green) you are aiming for. If you do not, you will not get close to your target (the hole). Always aim at a point on the green about 3 feet onto the green.*

~

ACKNOWLEDGEMENTS

To my Wife - I would like to thank you most of all for telling me to do what I love to do – Teach the game of Golf!

To the USGTF - for testing me and making sure I was ready and able to teach this game.

To Natural Golf - for giving me the change to teach the simplest swing in golf and the easiest one for my students to learn.

To Mr. Moe Norman - for inventing and perfecting the single plane swing.

To Mr. Jack Kuykendall – for foundering Natural Golf.

To Mr. Dale Hanson - for introducing me to the single plane swing.

To Mr. Ken Ellsworth (PGA) Director of Instruction, Natural Golf - for allowing me to teach with him and learn from him.

To Pineview Golf Club - for giving me my first job as a teaching Pro.

To Mr. Brady Godfrey (PGA) - Head Pro. Harbor Hills, Fl. for being my friend and allowing me to teach at his golf club and for his forward to this book.

To Mr. Mike Pullen (Owner) – for letting me teach at two of his golf clubs, St Augustine Shores and Cecil Field Golf Club.

To Mr. Jim Mc Cumber (Owner) - for letting me teach at his course, Westlands, Jacksonville, Fl.

To all the other Golf Clubs and all the Pro's that allowed me to come on their courses and teach all over this great Country.

To Mr. Ben Duncan (PGA) Head Pro. The Golf Club of Quincy - for letting me teach at your golf club.

To all the Natural Golf teaching professionals that I have known and learn from. Too many to name but you know who you are...Thanks guys

To my grandchildren Olivia "Puttin" and Colton "Pistol" Bridges – thanks for helping with the proofreading and their support with this book.

And to Mr. Bob Waller of Canada – my Editor – my friend and student – thank you for helping me with the editing of this book. Remember the word CONTACT! <u>Without you</u> there would be no book. I fell you have given much more than you got, Thanks Bob.

And last but certainly not least to all my students and friends- for having the faith in me as a Teacher and for you letting me take up your time, Thank you!

March 13, 2006

Billy J. Gaines, Sr.
511 Eloise St.
MacClenny, FL 32063

Dear Billy,

Greetings from sunny South Florida and the USGTF National Office!

We would like to congratulate you on having been chosen as one of the top WGTF teaching professionals. Please find enclosed our official publication regarding this occasion.

Out of the thousands of WGTF members, you are one of only 60 who were chosen as the top representatives of their profession. You were successful in undergoing a rigorous examination of not only your teaching ability, but your contributions to teaching and golf in general.

We hope you enjoy reading some of the interesting biographies from many of your peers throughout the world. Each teacher in the Top 60 is unique in his and her own right, with various ages, backgrounds, and nationalities represented. Despite these differences, what you all have in common is a love of the game, your dedication to your profession, and an outstanding ability to teach, communicate, and inspire your students.

We are very proud to honor you as part of the very first WGTF Top Teachers list. In years to come, as the WGTF continues its present state of growth, the list will inevitably be expanded. Therefore, your inclusion in this first list is an especially noteworthy achievement.

On behalf of the entire membership of the WGTF, I would like to wish you continued success in your golf teaching endeavors.

Sincerely,

Geoff Bryant,
President

To Whom It May Concern,

As of this date, I am no longer with Natural Golf. I have spent 13½ years with Natural Golf and it was a learning experience. I enjoyed my stay with the company, the staff, my fellow CI's and most of all the students I had met while teaching the Natural Golf Single Plane Swing, most I have been able to call "FRIEND".

It is not easy to give up my Teaching Certification with Natural Golf after all these Years- but I feel I have no choice! I have seen Natural Golf go through a lot of changes, from only having 26 instructors with Ken Ellsworth as its head instructor (with no money, just a dream) to a $20 million company and over 180 instructors. From going public - to going bankrupted!

Having it pass through difference owners - each trying so hard to make it a go because they, (like the certified instructors) believed in the swing of Mr. Moe Norman.

I still think the single plane swing that Mr. Norman swung is the most repeating swing in the game of golf! I will continue to play and teach it along with teaching the conventional swing. I wish the new owners all the best in their future but I feel I just can't stay with them.

If I can ever be of help to you or even if you just want to talk - please call or e-mail.

Till then..............Your Friend ....Bill

Billy J. Gaines Sr.